ČSA Czech Airlines
100 Years in the Air

JOZEF MOLS

AIRLINES SERIES, VOLUME 23

Front cover image: The only Airbus A330 to have entered service with the ČSA fleet. (Lukas Tochacek)

Back cover image: A ČSA Czech Airlines Boeing 737-500. (Ronald Vermeulen)

Title page image: A ČSA Czech Airlines Airbus A319. (Raymond Zammit)

Contents page image: A Tupolev Tu-134A from the Soviet-bloc period. (Alan Bushell)

Published by Key Books
An imprint of Key Publishing Ltd
PO Box 100
Stamford
Lincs PE9 1XP

www.keypublishing.com

The right of Jozef Mols to be identified as the
author of this book has been asserted in accordance
with the Copyright, Designs and Patents Act 1988
Sections 77 and 78.

Copyright © Jozef Mols, 2025

ISBN 978 1 80282 824 5

Typeset by SJmagic DESIGN SERVICES, India.

Contents

Introduction and Acknowledgements

How often does one have the opportunity to write a book about an airline that has celebrated its 100th birthday? ČSA Czech Airlines, established in 1923, is one of the five oldest airlines still existing in the world. At first, it operated only domestic routes but soon after, regional destinations were served. The carrier not only offered the population a fast and secure way of travel, but also acted as pacesetter for the local aircr industry by ordering aircraft built in Czechoslovakia.

In the 100 years of its existence, ČSA has had to weather many storms. Prior to World War Two, the airline had expanded its route network to include foreign destinations including Bucharest, Vienna and Moscow. It operated a fleet of modern aircraft, including the Douglas DC-2 and Fokker F.VII, and passengers were assisted during the flights by stewardesses. In 1938, however, Czechoslovakia had to cede its Sudetenland territory to Germany. In this way, ČSA lost several of its destinations. And when the rest of the country found itself occupied by German forces just prior to the outbreak of war in earnest, all operations ceased. A number of ČSA employees, including pilots and stewardesses, joined the domestic and foreign resistance, with many arrested, imprisoned and sentenced to death by the Germans. Therefore, once the war was over, the airline had to start up operations again with a decimated staff.

After the war, the country was pulled into the communist sphere of influence. This had repercussions on the composition of ČSA's fleet, which now included mostly Soviet-made aircraft. Also, destinations served by the carrier were often located within the Eastern Bloc. The first ČSA jet, a Tupolev Tu-104, landed in Prague on 2 November 1957.

It was not until 1989 that Czechoslovakia joined the free world again, to be reacquainted with the specific character of the capitalist system. The airline thus gained the opportunity to buy Western-made aircraft such as the Airbus A310, Boeing 737 and ATR propliners for domestic and regional services. In line with free-market policies, ČSA endeavoured to set up international alliances, with Air France becoming the carrier's first foreign shareholder. But when both ČSA and Air France ran into financial difficulties, the partnership ceased. Shortly afterwards, Czechoslovakia was divided into the Czech Republic and Slovakia, and the airline once again had to restructure its operations to cope with the new situation. ČSA Czechoslovak Airlines became ČSA Czech Airlines.

In 2001, ČSA joined the SkyTeam Alliance. Shortly after, the carrier rapidly expanded its international network and, by 2004, was serving 75 destinations in 44 countries worldwide, with a fleet of 45 aircraft. New Airbus A320s and A319s were ordered. At the same time, the first low-cost carriers entered the Czech market, and when the Czech Republic became a member of the European Union, this not only offered advantages but also caused some problems for the airline, as it had to renegotiate collective wage deals with its employees. All these events pushed ČSA's bookkeeping into the red. Therefore, the Czech government decided to launch a tender for the purchase of a major stake in the airline but, as it turned out, the deal did not materialise. In 2013, however, Korean Air would obtain a 44 per cent stake in ČSA. The contract with Airbus for the delivery of Airbus A320 and A319 jets signed earlier was cancelled. Instead, ČSA would order the more modern A320neo for delivery in 2019.

In 2017, Korean Air sold its stake in ČSA to Czech charter airline Travel Service, which later was rebranded as Smartwings.

At first, the change of ownership brought some positive results. But then, the COVID pandemic hit the world and airlines around the globe were grounded. Of course, this crisis had a financial impact on ČSA. In 2020, both ČSA and Smartwings had to file a motion with the Municipal Court in Prague to declare an extraordinary moratorium on debts. In sharp contrast with most other airlines around the world, ČSA did not benefit from any form of state aid during the crisis. Therefore, a major restructuring was necessary. ČSA was saved from bankruptcy when new shareholders, including Prague City Air, invested in the struggling carrier. With a fleet of only two remaining aircraft, operations were started again.

Acknowledgements

In this book, the author endeavours to provide some insight into the history of this remarkable airline. This publication has only been possible thanks to the assistance of several people. Therefore, the author wishes to thank all photographers who allowed him to use their photographs, as well as the aviation historians, libraries, research institutions and specialised aviation journalists who provided access to their documentation. He also wishes to express his gratitude to his partner, Marianne Van Leuvenhaege, for encouraging him to write this book and for proofreading the manuscript. And of course his gratitude also goes to Key Books for publishing and distributing this book.

Wommelgem, Belgium,
1 August 2024

Chapter 1

Beginnings

The origins of Czech aviation can be traced back to the early days of the 20th century, before the time when the Czech Republic even existed. Indeed, the area was still part of the Austro-Hungarian Empire when local designers Jan Kaspar and his cousin Evžen Čihák started building their first aeroplane in Pardubice, the town where Kaspar was born. Kaspar had graduated from the Czechoslovak Technical University in Prague and had continued his studies in Germany, where he concentrated on aircraft engine construction.[1]

In 1909, Kaspar started the construction of his first aircraft, which was inspired by Antoinette, the aircraft model of French designer Hubert Latham. During construction, Kaspar learned about French aviator Louis Blériot's successful flight from Calais to Dover. Disillusionment followed when Kaspar's first aircraft was not able to take off. Not deterred, Kaspar decided to buy a Blériot XI, which he equipped with an engine of his own design. Later, he switched the engine for an Anzani. He would make his first successful flight on 16 April 1910, during which he flew 2km (1¼ miles) at a height of 20–25m (approximately 65ft). The achievement made Kaspar the first Czechoslovak pilot. A year later, Kaspar managed to build another aircraft, which he called JK. Its first test flight took place on 30 April 1911, from Pardubice to Chrudim and back. That same day, Kaspar made the first flight with a passenger as he carried his cousin Čihák. He would make his most famous flight on 13 May 1911, when he travelled from Pardubice to Velká Chuchle (a distance of 121km or 76 miles). At that time, it was the longest flight ever recorded in the Austro-Hungarian Empire. (The aircraft can now be seen in the National Technical Museum in Prague.) Together with his brother, Kaspar registered the first aircraft manufacturing company in Pardubice. Unfortunately, his last years would be marked by personal tragedy and financial hardship, as he lost all of his financial resources following World War One. Suffering from mental illness, he committed suicide in Pardubice in 1927.

As in many other countries, transportation of mail and packages provided an impetus to further develop transportation by air. Just before the end of World War One, the Austro-Hungarian postal administration established the first air mail line between Vienna, Krakow and Lemberg (today's Lviv in Ukraine), which was later extended to Kiev. Flights were operated with Hansa Brandenburg Br.CI aircraft, powered by an Austro-Daimler engine of 160 hp. Although the postal services did not plan a stop in what would become Czechoslovakia, special collection centres for airmail were set up in Prague and Brno. As a newly independent country in 1918, Czechoslovakia necessitated new approaches to establish an air transportation system. In order to start up such activities, the postal services needed aircraft, airports, pilots and maintenance staff. Therefore, the postal services asked for assistance from the army, which had been gradually acquiring aircraft and equipment and had also built some airfields. At that time, the military used Hansa Brandenburg, Ansaldo SVA 10, Phoenix CI, Oeffag C.II, Aviatik C1 and Anatra DS Anasal aircraft. Later on, Rumplers and Fokker D.VII aircraft were obtained. France donated several aircraft as well, including Spads, Salmson Sal, Farman F.60 Goliaths and a Breguet XIV. But the first flight, carrying postal packages and mail on 13 July 1919, was operated by a Czech-built Aero aircraft. This flight was carried out for publicity purposes as part of a broader campaign to promote the establishment of postal air transport.

In co-operation with the army, other mail flights were operated along a strategic line Prague–Bratislava–Lucenec–Uzhorod. These flights were operated most of the time by Brandenburg aircraft, which could carry up to 50kg (110lb) of mail. Due to operational difficulties and lack of resources, however, these flights had ceased as early as 20 October 1919. After the establishment of an international air transport organisation in 1919, the Czechoslovak Ministry of Public Works was entrusted with the task of organising air transportation along new routes made necessary by the country's altered geography by comparison with when the area was was part of Austria-Hungary. Under the former empire, the main transport routes had been between Vienna and Prague and between Budapest and Bratislava, the main centres of economic and political activity. Now the independent Czechoslovakia would have to establish links from west, i.e. the new capital at Prague, to east. The resulting air mail routes from Prague duly commenced, but were still operated by the Air Transport Department on behalf of the Ministry of Posts and Telegraphs. All routes operated were domestic, but international connections were also considered. However, it would not be a Czechoslovak airline that would start up such international flights. A debut international route was opened by the French-Romanian CERNA (Compagnie Franco-Roumaine de Transport Aérienne). The airline made its first mail flight on 5 October 1920, and started operating a regular service between Paris and Prague via Strasbourg from 15 October of the same year. Later on, this service was extended to include Warsaw and, even later, Vienna and Budapest. CERNA had been established in April 1920 by French fighter pilot Pierre Claret de Fleurieu and the Banca Marmorosh, Blank & Co from Romania. On the Paris–Strasbourg–Prague route, the airline used French-built Potez aircraft.[2]

The same year, two modest Czechoslovak airlines were established. Ikarus was founded by Josef Gürl, and First Prague Airlines Falco was founded by Julius Arigi. The two companies operated a fleet of modified older military aircraft, such as the Aero A.14 Brandenburg with Hiero or Daimler engine and the Albatros D.II for mail transport. Their activities consisted only of sightseeing flights and aerial acrobatics; occasionally, they carried one or two passengers. Nevertheless, the impact of these companies should not be underestimated. In 1920 alone, Ikarus transported some 5,600 passengers during 2,800 flights. The airline considered offering regular air transport, for which it obtained a Smolik S-1a aeroplane, and test flights commenced on the Prague–Strasbourg–Paris route. However, because of competition by CERNA, it was decided that Ikarus would concentrate its attention on a Prague–Brno–Bratislava–Uzhorod route and later on the Prague–Vienna route. A little later, Richard Harabus would set up another airline, Aero-Lloyd.

In 1921, Ikarus and Falco decided to merge, becoming Čs-LAS (Czechoslovak Aviation Joint Stock Company) in an aim to strengthen the carriers' position in the face of competition from CERNA and Aero-Lloyd. Arigi, soon left the merged company and set up his own enterprise, Marianske Lazne Aviation Company.[3] With the support of many Czechoslovak politicians, he hoped to be assigned the planned Prague–Bratislava–Uzhorod and Prague–Vienna routes, and therefore ordered several Aero A.10 aircraft. However, the Prague–Vienna route was assigned to CERNA, which started operations on 1 May 1922, using Potez IX aircraft. Čs-LAS would now have to concentrate its attention on connections across the republic. The start of such flights was announced in the press, stating that modern Aero A.10 aircraft would be used as of 1 March 1923. Unfortunately, the airline announced shortly thereafter that it had declared bankruptcy and was in liquidation. The A.10 aircraft were taken over by the newly established Czechoslovak State Airlines, which was also starting operations at that time. During 1923 and 1924, the aircraft would be used on the Prague–Bratislava route, which was later extended to include Košice. All hopes of a private domestic airline setting up air transportation were dashed.

At the end of February 1923, the Ministry of National Defence and the Ministry of Public Works reached an agreement to organise air transportation. The Aero factory was ordered to modify Hansa Brandenburg B.I aircraft to be used for air transport, and these aircraft would now be known as the Aero A.14 and Aero A.15. On 1 March 1923, the Air Transport Department started flights on the Prague–Bratislava–Kosice route with Aero A.14 L-BARA. Three more Letov S-1 aircraft flew an escort. Although the plane was damaged during the landing in Bratislava, it was repaired in time for a successful return flight.

Above: Jan Kaspar's 1911 monoplane in the Technical Museum in Prague. (Alan Wilson, CC BY-SA 2.0 hu.wikipedia.org/wiki/Jan_Ka%C5%A1par#/media/F%C3%A1jl:1911_Kaspar_Monoplane_(8191429766).jpg)

Left: An Aero A-10 that would serve until June 1924. (Aero Vodochody, public domain)

Below: An Aero A-14. (ČSA, public domain)

Above: A postcard showing a Blériot Spad of the Compagnie Franco-Roumaine, used on routes via Czechoslovakia. (Editions Dubernet, public domain en.m.wikipedia.org/wiki/File:Avion_Berline_Spad.jpg)

Right: A poster of the Compagnie Franco-Roumaine, showing flights to Budapest via Prague. (Compagnie Franco-Roumaine de navigation aérienne – public domain en.m.wikipedia.org/wiki/File:Affiche_Compagnie_Franco_Roumaine_de_navigation_a%C3%A9rienne.jpg)

Chapter 2

Czechoslovak State Airlines

After several unsuccessful attempts by private companies, the Czechoslovak government took the initiative and organised civil domestic air transport. This process was entrusted to the Ministry of National Defence, which created a 'transport detachment' on 29 July 1923. Military aircraft were operated by military pilots and looked after by military mechanics, but it was soon decided that the transport detachment should be transformed into a state airline. Thus was founded Czechoslovak State Airlines on 6 October, with the scope of the airline limited to the territory of Czechoslovakia. Major Hupner was appointed as its first director. The ceremonial opening of business took place on the day of the celebration of the fifth anniversary of the founding of the Czechoslovak Republic. That day, 28 October 1923, saw Captain Karl Brabance (who would later become chief pilot of ČSA) make a symbolic flight around Kbely Airport in an Aero A.14 aircraft (L-BARC). A day later, he took off in this aircraft once again with Vàclav König, a journalist from the daily *Lidové Noviny*. Besides the passenger, the aircraft was also transporting 15kg (33lb) of newspapers and some mail. The aircraft flew the Prague–Bratislava route, a journey of some 320km (198 miles). The same day, another Aero A.14 (L-BARI), piloted by Staff Sergeant-Major Josef Cinibulk, took off in the opposite direction from Bratislava's Vajnory Airport, heading for Prague Kbely. As with the first flight from Prague, this flight also had a journalist on board, Gustav Adolf Bezo. Notwithstanding these experimental flights, regular air transport of people, cargo and mail did not start until 3 March 1924. Later on, the line was extended to include Košice, by which time Aero A.10 aircraft had been introduced. In 1926, the route was once again extended, to serve Brno. Around that time, de Havilland DH.50 aircraft, accommodating four passengers, were introduced. When the Prague–Mariánské Lázně line was opened, it was an immediate success. From 1925, the flight was operated by the Aero factory itself, which had obtained a transport concession. Passengers were transported in the open cabin of an Aero A.11. In 1927, Czechoslovak State Airlines took over the route.

In the meantime, another airline was also established. Thanks to a government subsidy, the Skoda plants set up the Czechoslovak Aviation Company. This was a joint stock company that was also based in Prague, and at first only represented foreign airlines that flew to Prague. In 1928, however, it would start up its own operations. In March of that year, an international service was launched, connecting Vienna via Prague to Dresden and Berlin. A few months later, the Prague–Mariánské Lázně-Kassel–Rotterdam route was inaugurated, and in 1929, Nuremberg was added to the route network. Later on, this operation was routed to Rotterdam via Leipzig, Dortmund and Essen and in 1931, it was extended to include Amsterdam. That same year, flights to Zürich and Basel via Munich were introduced.

Czechoslovakia now decided to change its civil aircraft markings. Rules for marking civil aircraft had been introduced during the 1919 Paris Convention, and aircraft from Czechoslovakia had been allocated the L-B registration mark. This mark was based on the call signs used for radio communications under the London Radiotelegraph Convention of 1912. After the amendment of the international aviation regulations for radio operation and approval by the Czechoslovak government in 1929, L-B was replaced by OK. There is one widespread legend told of the curious manner behind the adoption of this mark. The Czechoslovak delegation had arrived late at the convention and discovered that the previously agreed mark of CS had already been taken, chosen by the Portuguese in honour of King Carlos. The Czechoslovak delegation thus had to improvise and reserve a new mark. Since the delegation was headed by Otakar Koudelka, someone suggested using his initials as the official mark. But it could just as easily have been Otakar Kaspar, hypothetically related to the pioneer of Czech aviation, Jan Kaspar. Nobody knows for sure. Nevertheless, the proposal was accepted and the OK-mark came into being on Czechoslovak civil aircraft with effect from 1 January 1930.[1]

While Czechoslovakia's airlines were rapidly expanding their route networks, there was also significant technological progress in the construction of aircraft. Canvas and wood had been replaced by metal, so aeroplanes became larger and heavier. As a result, engines had to evolve in turn. Since 1928, these were no longer started by hand but rather by compressed air, which was safer. At the same time, aircraft ranges had been extended and the number of seats had been increased. Czechoslovak State Airlines then extended its routes to Zagreb (Yugoslavia) and, in 1934, obtained a Saunders & Roe (SARO) A-19 Cloud amphibious aircraft, which transported passengers onward from Zagreb to the island of Susak, where it landed at sea. This run thus became known as the Adriatic Express. Meanwhile, Fokker F.VII aircraft were used on the routes to Cluj and Bucharest in Romania. Later on, a flight between Bratislava and Vienna was inaugurated. In the meantime, ČSA's aircraft had been fitted with radio equipment, enabling them to fly under Instrument Flight Rules (IFR) at night or under reduced visibility. In 1934, ČSA introduced its new logo: a silhouette of a swallow flying in a circle from right to left with the word 'ČSA' at the top. This logo would be used until the start of World War Two.

In 1936, ČSA started operating a second international route from Prague via Uzhorod to Cluj-Napoca and Bucharest, nicknamed the Romanian Express. Earlier, a domestic route linking Prague to Moravská Ostrava via Hradec Kralove had been opened. A third international route linked Piestany with Vienna via Bratislava. In 1936, ČSA added another international route from Prague via Uzhorod, Iași, Kiev and Bryansk to Moscow Tusino in the Soviet Union. Flights to Moscow were operated by British Airspeed AS-6 Envoy aircraft with two Walter Castor II engines of 176kW each, and with a capacity of six passengers. That year, ČSA was the second airline in Europe (after KLM) to purchase Douglas DC-2 aircraft, which could seat up to 14 passengers. In the next two years, the venerable Douglas DC-3 was also added to the fleet. These aircraft were very popular and earned the name Flying Pullmans. The introduction of the Dakota came as a real revelation, as the aircraft were equipped with on-board sights and radio compasses, automatic pilots, de-icing equipment and retractable landing gear. Passenger comfort was enhanced by the addition of toilets, comfortable heated cabins and, for the first time, flight attendants, who made their debut aboard ČSA's planes in 1937.

With the introduction of new and more modern aircraft, the service level was increased. By the 1920s, passengers could ask for a drop of alcohol to warm them up when flying in an aircraft with an open cabin. Starting in 1936, refreshments were offered, which could be ordered in advance and then picked up at the airport prior to boarding the flight. In 1937, when air stewardesses became part of ČSA's services, refreshments were served in the air. The first passengers to enjoy such luxury were those flying on the Prague–Bratislava–Klagenfurt–Trieste–Venice route, known as the Riviera Express. The offer included sandwiches and cakes, as well as hot broth, tea or coffee, Pilsner beer or champagne, all served in glass and porcelain.[2]

Besides the Douglas aircraft, ČSA was also using three-engined Fokker F.IX D aircraft licence-built by Avia, which could carry up to 17 passengers. The last type of aircraft with which ČSA modernised its fleet before the war was the Italian Savoia-Marchetti S.73. These modern and elegant aircraft could carry 18 passengers and four crew members. ČSA obtained six (OK-BAB, OK-BAC, OK-BAD, OK-BAE, OK-BAF and OK-BAG) and from 1937 till 1939, deployed them on regular flights to Paris, Rome, Budapest and Brussels.[3]

In the first half of the 1930s, a trend from the United States began to spread in Europe, with the aim of making air travel more pleasant for passengers. June 1937 saw ČSA introduce its first stewardesses to crew the new Savoia-Marchettis. In June 1937, Marie Stara, Marie Müllerova and Hana Fuchsova were hired, followed by Maria Terezia Thurn-Taxis. The stewardesses were known in Czech as 'letuskas', but ČSA simultaneously organised contests among passengers to come up with new names for these young ladies. Many suggestions were received, including air maid, flight cookie, flight maiden, cloud mama, etc, but 'letuska' remained the most popular. Although the job of stewardess was considered an attractive profession, admired by many, there were also those who condemned it as an excess of female emancipation. The stewardess not only kept the passengers company, but also helped with check-in, provided medical assistance if needed, acted as an interpreter and, of course, served the highly popular refreshments. There were high requirements of stewardesses. They had to be under 25 and show excellent fitness and health. The selected candidates had to undergo a physical, psychological and technological examination at the garrison hospital in Prague. Their language skills were highly appreciated; when not flying, they worked at ČSA's offices, especially on English and French correspondence. However, maintaining correspondence with passengers after their flight was greatly frowned upon.[4]

Unfortunately, in 1938 there was an accident involving Savoia-Marchetti OK-BAG. The aircraft was flying a scheduled flight from Prague to Paris, but crashed in the German Black Forest in bad weather. All passengers and the entire crew perished.

Aero A-14 Brandenburg L-BARI of Czechoslovak State Airlines. (ČSA, public domain)

In 1926, four-passenger de Havilland DH-50 aircraft entered the fleet. (Jozef Mols collection)

Right: Between 1924 and 1927, this Farman Goliath – a converted French bomber – was used on the route from Prague via Kosice to Brno. (ČSA archives, public domain)

Below: This Farman F.62 Goliath arrived at Brno Airport on 23 May 1926, to open the Brno–Prague route. (Brno Turany Airport Archive)

This Aero A.23 was used on the route from Prague to Mariánské Lázně. (ČSA Archives, public domain)

This Aero A.35 was used in Susak on the Adriatic Express. (Aero Vodochody, public domain)

The Avia BH-25 was first offered to ČSA, but the company chose not to buy the plane. Instead, the aircraft entered the fleet of ČSA's competitor Skoda. (Photographer unknown, public domain, commons.wikimedia.org/wiki/File:Avia_BH-25_s_motorem_Jupiter_IV.jpg)

In 1934, this Saunders & Roe (SARO) A-19 Cloud joined the fleet and was used on the Zagreb to Susak route. (VHU.cz Military History Museum Prague, public domain)

The Airspeed AS-6 Envoy powered by Walter Castor II engines was used on flights to Moscow Tushino. (Photographer unknown, public domain, en.m.wikipedia.org/wiki/File:Walter_Castor_II_a_Airspeed_AS.6E_ Envoy_III_(OK-BAL).jpg)

The Airspeed AS-6, used on the route to Moscow, could transport up to six passengers. (Photographer unknown, public domain, commons.wikimedia.org/wiki/File:Airspeed_Envoy_u_%C4%8CSA_(1935).jpg)

Above: ČSA's Avia Fokker
F-IXD aircraft could carry up to
17 passengers. (ETH Library
Zürich, public domain)

Right: Passengers boarding a ČSA
Fokker aircraft. (Photographer
unknown, public domain,
commons.wikimedia.org/wiki/
Category:Avia_F-IX#/media/
File:Avia_Fokker_F-IXD_a_Walter_
Pegas_II-M2_(1935).jpg)

ČSA also added Douglas DC-3 aircraft to its fleet. Preserved outside the ČSA HQ building in the middle of Prague Airport, this is actually a pre-war DC-3-229, msn 1995, which was delivered new to Panagra as NC18119 on 19 October 1937. It saw no military service and was eventually flown to Prague for preservation in June 1991. Oddly enough, the original OK-XDM still exists and is on display at a museum in France! (Alan Wilson, Creative Commons Attribution-Share Alike 2.0 Generic, en.m.wikipedia.org/wiki/File:Douglas_DC3-229_OK-XDM_%28823 0123433%29.jpg)

A ČSA Douglas DC-3 Dakota bringing a Czech delegation to Zürich. (ETH Library Zürich – public domain)

A ČSA Douglas DC-3 is towed away. (Jozef Mols collection)

A ČSA Savoia-Marchetti SM.73 seen at the airport. (ČSA archives, public domain)

Arrival of a ČSA Savoia-Marchetti SM.73 at Prague Airport. (ČSA archives, public domain)

Fokker F-IXD, built under licence by Avia in Czechoslovakia. (ČSA archives, public domain)

Chapter 3

War

By the late 1930s, ČSA had established itself among the most important European airlines. Between 1924 and the end of 1938, it had carried 139,735 passengers. On some routes, the airline operated independently, while on others, it co-operated with other airlines. A good example of this co-operation is the 'Romanian Express', on which ČSA flew passengers from Prague to Bucharest with stops in Uzhhorod and Cluj. Romanian carrier SARTA operated on the same route, in what we would now call a code-share agreement with ČSA. In July 1937, ČSA also started co-operation with Romanian airlines LARES (Liniile Aeriene Exploatate cu Statul). The 'bread and butter' operations of ČSA, however, consisted of the route from London via Brussels to Prague, Piestany and Cluj, connecting with a flight to Bucharest. On this transEuropean express, it was ČSA, SABENA and LARES that co-operated.

Due to the expansion of ČSA operations, and the fact that the military also used Kbely Airport in Prague, the airline's infrastructure became too limited. Expansion of the airport was ruled out, so the Ministry of Public Works decided, in 1930, to build a new civil airport in Prague. A site near the village of Ruzyně was selected and, after eight years of construction, the new Prague-Ruzyně Airport opened in 1938. The airport was equipped only with grass runways and a paved apron connected to the handling areas in front of the hangars, but it soon became clear that the runways were unsuitable for the increasingly larger and heavier aircraft, so the construction of a reinforced runway started. By 1938, ČSA guaranteed the connection of Prague to more than 100 cities, in co-operation with 17 foreign airlines.

By that time, however, dark clouds were gathering over Europe. Germany started a low-intensity undeclared war on Czechoslovakia on 17 September 1938. In order to appease German dictator Adolf Hitler, some great European powers (including the United Kingdom and France) formally asked Czechoslovakia to cede its Sudetenland territory to Germany in the hope of avoiding direct war with Germany. France had signed a military pact with the Czechoslovak Republic and was bound, under the articles of this agreement, to defend the country against a Nazi invasion.

The Sudetenland was a strip of land near the German and Austrian borders, but when the Czechoslovak Republic had been established at the end of World War One, its mostly German-speaking inhabitants had not been consulted whether they wished to be citizens of the new country. And although the Czechoslovak constitution guaranteed equality for all citizens, there was a tendency among political leaders to transform the country into an instrument of Czech and Slovak nationalism. German-speaking inhabitants of the Sudetenland had been under-represented in the government and the army. Moreover, the Great Depression impacted the highly industrialised and export-oriented Sudeten Germans more than it did the Czech and Slovak populations. By 1936, 60 per cent of the unemployed people in Czechoslovakia were German-speaking.[1] In 1933, Sudeten German leader Konrad Henlein had founded the Sudeten German Party (SdP), which was militantly nationalist and openly hostile to the Czechoslovak government. It is not clear whether the SdP was a Nazi front organisation from its beginning or evolved into one later, but by 1935, it was the second-largest political party in Czechoslovakia, concentrating the German-speakers' votes, whereas Czech and Slovak votes were spread among several parties. Shortly after the *Anschluss* of Austria with Germany, Henlein met with Hitler in Berlin on 28 March 1938. The Sudeten German leader was instructed to make demands that would be unacceptable to the Czechoslovak government, which was led by President Edvard Benes. A few weeks later, the SdP gained

88 per cent of the ethnic German votes. Although in a secret letter Benes offered Hitler some 2,300sq mi of the Sudetenland on the condition that Germany would admit 1.5–2 million Sudeten Germans that Czechoslovakia would expel, Hitler never replied.[2]

After France and the United Kingdom had urged Czechoslovakia to cede Sudetenland in the face of German pressure, an agreement was concluded in Munich on 30 September 1938, by Germany, the United Kingdom, the French Republic and fascist Italy. The agreement provided for the German annexation of the Sudetenland. Neither Czechoslovakia nor the Soviet Union, two countries with representatives present in Munich, were invited to the conference. A little later, neighbouring Hungary and Poland also wished to 'reincorporate' strips of Czechoslovak territory close to their common borders. On 2 November, the First Vienna Award was signed, separating largely Hungarian-inhabited territories in southern Slovakia and southern Subcarpathian Rus from Czechoslovakia. On 30 November, Czechoslovakia also ceded to Poland small patches of land in the Spiš and Orava regions. As a result of the Munich Agreement and other claims by its neighbours, Czechoslovakia lost its airports at Liberec, Karlovy Vary, Mariánské Lázně, Košice and Uzhhorod and ČSA had to cancel flights to these cities. Still, the Czechoslovak Council of Ministers instructed ČSA to maintain winter air traffic on the Prague–Paris and Prague–Brussels routes and to replace the route to Uzhhorod by one linking Prague with Slatinske Doly.

Half a year later, on 15 March 1939, German troops occupied the remaining territory of the Czechoslovak Republic, turning it into the Protectorate of Bohemia and Moravia. The Slovaks simultaneously achieved the creation of an independent Slovak state under control of Germany. By decision of the Reich Chancellery, the 'Reich Aviation Law' entered into force on 26 April 1939, according to which, only Deutsche Lufthansa could operate air transport in Germany and the occupied territories. All ČSA aircraft were taken over by the Germans. At that time, the fleet included five Savoia Marchetti SM-73 aircraft, four twin-engined Airspeed AS-6 Envoys, two three-engined Fokker/Avia F.IX, four three-engined Fokker/Avia F.VIIb-3m and one amphibious Saro SR-19 Cloud. Ruzyně Airport was occupied and some of the aircraft were taken over by Deutsche Lufthansa while others were dismantled.

The German occupation would last for six years. A number of ČSA employees, including pilots and stewardesses, joined the domestic and foreign resistance and many were subsequently arrested, imprisoned and sentenced to death. The Czechoslovak government had managed to leave the country and would set up a 'government in exile' in London.

Chapter 4

A Difficult New Start

When World War Two came to an end, it was obvious that Czechoslovakia had to reactivate its national airline, but this was not an easy task. Many former ČSA employees had died whilst fighting at the front or in the national resistance movement. Even before the end of the war, the Czechoslovak government-in-exile took part in negotiations that would lead to the creation of the International Civil Aviation Organisation (ICAO) and the reorganisation of the International Air Transport Association (IATA).

Near the end of the war, the Czech population revolted against the Nazi German occupation forces during the Prague uprising. Fighting was going on in the streets as the population was encouraged by the knowledge that liberation forces were closing in on the city. At that time, Ruzyně Airport was used by a German SS detachment. Realising that they would soon have to retreat, the SS tried to destroy the infrastructure, but local residents and airport workers intervened. The airport had never been bombed during the war, as Allied pilots had focused on destroying German aircraft. Therefore, the airport was more or less preserved for a rapid post-war restoration of air traffic. During the war, the Luftwaffe had seen the need to reinforce the runways to accommodate its heavy aircraft. As a result, the airport was actually in a better state than before the war. Of course, several wrecks of German aircraft, which had been damaged during bombing raids, had to be removed. One airworthy Junkers Ju 52/3m, however, was found among the wreckage. It was transported to the Letov factory, where it was prepared for passenger flights. Soon, more aircraft of the same type would be repaired by the same factory. It is believed a total of 13 Junkers Ju 52/3M could be rehabilitated in this way. Another aircraft type left behind by the Germans was the twin-engine transport and trainer Siebel Si 204, production of which had been transferred by Siebel Flugzeugwerke to the Aero and ČKD Praha factories. Not only did Czechoslovakia restore a number of ex-Luftwaffe Siebels, but production of this aircraft continued after the war under the designation of Aero C-103. ČSA would use several on its domestic network between 1947 and 1951, though Sub-Carpathian Ruthenia was no longer an option for travel, this region having been annexed by the Soviet Union in 1945. There was also a single Junkers Ju 352 Hercules aircraft among the German stocks left behind and, although it was damaged, the Air Transport Group managed to put it back in service. But it would only perform a single flight from Prague to Moscow. On board was a new car, manufactured in Czechoslovakia, which was given to Stalin as a present.

On 4 August 1945, a Lisunov Li-2 aircraft, operated by Soviet airline Aeroflot, landed at Ruzyně Airport, intended to begin service on a Prague–Warsaw–Minsk–Moscow route. Nearly a month later the Swedish airline ABA Aerotransport started up flights on the Prague–Stockholm route. A Prague–London flight was also initiated, using converted American bombers, while mail was brought to the British capital by Mosquito bombers. The US Air Force started flights on a Vienna–Prague–Frankfurt route, while Air France commenced operations in Prague with a Junkers Ju 52/3m aircraft, linking Prague with Paris via Strasbourg. Yugoslav military aviation units simultaneously started up a Prague–Belgrade route, which was later taken over by the civilian airline Aeroput (which would later become JAT). The first aircraft with the Czechoslovak flag on its tail took off on 28 August 1945 for a flight from Ruzyně to Moscow.

On 14 September 1945, the Czechoslovak government decided that all air transport within the country would in the future be operated by a single national enterprise, known as Czechoslovak Airlines. At the same time, the Slovak joint-stock company that had been set up during the war and was also flying aircraft with the 'OK' registration, was abolished. After its re-establishment in 1946, ČSA made its first commercial flight on the Prague–Zürich route on 1 March of that year. Three days later, the route to Paris (via Strasbourg) was inaugurated, while flights to Vienna, Budapest, Belgrade and Sofia also started. Later on, destinations including Amsterdam and Stockholm were added, sometimes in co-operation with foreign airlines such as KLM, ABA and Air France. ČSA only had three Junkers Ju 52/3m aircraft at its disposal to operate these flights, so it was decided to purchase 25 Douglas DC-47 aircraft from US Army war surplus. Once modified for passenger transport, these aircraft could be seen on the Prague–Brno–Bratislava route. In June 1946, Pan American World Airways replaced the USAF on the flights between Prague and New York, using Lockheed Constellation aircraft. The first of these flights was routed from New York via Gander, Shannon, London, Brussels and Prague to Vienna. On 8 August 1946, the newly established British European Airways (BEA) launched its London–Prague line in pool with ČSA and, later on, ČSA and Sabena would start up a Prague–Brussels route in a similar way. LOT and ČSA co-operated on a Prague–Warsaw route whereas Danish DDL initiated flights to Prague on 3 August 1946. In co-operation with the Romanian-Soviet airline TARS, flights to Bucharest were launched. In the space of about a year, ČSA had managed to start up flights to some ten foreign destinations as well as objectives within its borders.

ČSA took to the skies again with its fleet of Ju 52/3M and Douglas Dakota aircraft. But it also introduced, for a very short time, a Hodek Hk-101, which was designed in secrecy during the war. In 1942, Vincenc Hodek, the owner of aircraft instrument maker V Hodek Praha, and Stanislav Kriz, began work on the design of a small twin-engined sports plane. To avoid German attention, design work was carried out in secret during the night in Hodek's apartment. Construction of a prototype started immediately after the war in a rented workshop in Libeň (Prague), with Hodek recruiting experienced technicians from the recently disbanded German Junkers and Škoda-Kauba companies. The prototype was completed in the summer of 1947 and was presented to ČSA for evaluation. Since the Hk-101 was a two-seater, it could only be used for mail services. After a few months of evaluation, ČSA returned the aircraft to the designer without placing an order.[1]

After the war, Czechoslovakia drifted slowly but surely into the communist sphere of influence. The Western Allies had failed to liberate Prague, which was seen as emblematic of a lack of concern for Czechoslovakia that had first been demonstrated by the Munich Agreement. It was not forgotten that Stalin had opposed this agreement and that Prague had been liberated by the Red Army. Hungarian historian Stephen Kertesz wrote that 'American forces had remained a cowardly or cynical onlooker while Prague was struggling for life'.[2] British diplomat Sir Orme Sargent wrote that 'the Prague uprising was the moment that Czechoslovakia was definitely lost to the West'.[3]

In spite of the uprising, it was the Yalta Conference that decided the future of Czechoslovakia. The conference took place in this Soviet resort town in the Crimea from 4–11 February 1945. Present were US President Franklin D. Roosevelt, British Prime Minister Winston Churchill and Soviet Premier Josef Stalin. There, they made important decisions about the future progress of the war and the post-war world. Not only the future of Germany was discussed, but the Americans and British generally agreed that future governments in Eastern European nations bordering the Soviet Union should be friendly to the Soviet regime, while the Soviets pledged to allow free elections in all territories they had liberated from Nazi Germany.[4]

For ČSA, the negative influence of Soviet intervention was visible in both the composition of the fleet and the establishment of air routes to mostly communist countries or countries within the Soviet sphere of influence. On the other hand, Western countries also restricted flights to Prague, and prohibited ČSA flights over their territories, while the United States declared an embargo on the supply of planes and spare parts for the Dakotas. However, the Czechoslovak technicians found a way to obtain construction plans for the Dakota and were able to manufacture spare parts, in this way keeping the aircraft in the air. One of these aircraft, Douglas DC-3 OK-WDI, even made a test flight from Prague to Bombay. In 1948, ČSA still showed some interest in obtaining American Douglas DC-4 aircraft, but this idea had to be abandoned once it became clear that the US was not willing to export such aircraft to communist countries.

At the end of the war, the Luftwaffe left behind several damaged Junkers Ju 52-3m aircraft, which were repaired and put back in service by ČSA. (Jozef Mols collection, public domain)

A ČSA Junkers Ju 52 seen at Zürich Airport. (ETH Bibliothek Zürich, public domain)

The Junkers Ju 52 were used on both domestic and regional services. (ETH Bibliothek Zürich, public domain)

A Junkers Ju 52-3m at Prague Airport. (Radio Prague, public domain)

For a while, ČSA evaluated the Hodek HK-101, but an order was never placed. (Jozef Mols collection, public domain)

Two more views of the Hodek HK-101. (Jozef Mols collection, public domain)

Above: A ČSA Aero C-103A at Prague Airport. (Radio Prague, public domain)

Left: The Aero C-103 was a German aircraft, built under German control in Czechoslovakia, but after the war, Aero would continue its production for ČSA. (Radio Prague, public domain)

A single Junkers Ju 352 Hercules remained at the Prague Airport at the end of the war and was used by ČSA to transport a car made in Czechoslovakia to Moscow as a gift to Josef Stalin. (Radio Prague, public domain)

Chapter 5

The Communist Coup

In February 1948, the democratic government of Czechoslovakia was toppled by a communist coup d'état. Following the coup, the country would become a socialist state aligned with the Soviet Union. The new government tried to falsify history by discrediting the Czech resistance during World War Two, considering it a threat to communist legitimacy. Furthermore, the role of the working class in the Czech uprising against the Nazi occupation was overstated and the number of Soviet soldiers killed during the liberation of Czechoslovakia was inflated. Several former resistance leaders were arrested. In the tense atmosphere following the events in February, many experienced pilots and employees had to leave or were fired, and at the same time there was a huge wave of emigration which would result in a series of hijackings. For a while, air transport continued to operate, thanks to previous deployments, but rapidly declined thereafter. A number of routes, mostly domestic but especially international ones were terminated. Of the original 22 international routes served in 1947, only half remained by 1951 and only seven a year later. Western airlines would also significantly reduce flights to Prague, with some countries revoking permission for Czechoslovak aircraft to fly over their airspace. In May 1948, Czechoslovak Airlines became a state enterprise. As a result of the new political and economic orientation towards the USSR, the airline would add Soviet-built aircraft to its fleet instead of the new Douglas DC-6 or Lockheed Constellation aircraft that were originally considered, commencing a long era of reliance on Soviet technology.[1]

Shortly after the coup, the Soviet Union delivered ten Ilyushin Il-12 aircraft, each with 18 seats. ČSA was not completely satisfied with these aircraft, but had no choice but to accept them. A little later, seven Lisunov Li-2 aircraft joined the ČSA fleet. These were otherwise Douglas DC-3 aircraft, built under licence in the Soviet Union. These could seat 22 passengers. The Ilyushin Il-14, capable of transporting 24 passengers, was also introduced and would become the backbone of the ČSA fleet. Before long, Prague's Avia factory started licence production of the type, making a series of modifications to improve performance and increase capacity to 42 seats. Several routes, served prior to the coup, were suspended, but now new destinations were added to the network including Berlin, Venice, Gothenburg, Haifa, Helsinki, Lydda, Milan, Nice, Sofia, Tel Aviv and Trieste were new destinations. Over all, though, the number of passengers and the revenue of the airline saw a decline. At the same time, Bata Shoes' aviation section had been nationalised and was renamed Svitlet[2]. In 1951, ČSA took over Svitlet and started up taxi flights with this new branch. Before the takeover, Czechoslovakia had the densest air taxi network in the world, with 16 permanent bases and 80 additional destinations, which most of the time were mostly located at flying club airfields. Under ČSA's control, Svitlet used a fleet of Aero 45 aircraft. ČSA also set up another subsidiary, Agrolet, which was in charge of agricultural work. Another strategy by the airline to compensate for lost revenue due to the decline in passenger numbers was to resume the transportation of mail and newspapers around the country. A slow thaw in international relations started in 1955 with a gradual renewal of international routes. ČSA restored its flights to Moscow with a stopover in Vilnius, and introduced a direct route to Paris.

In the second half of the 1950s, jet airliners made their entry into the fleets of major airlines around the world. The Soviet Union, which wanted to show off its leadership in this area as proof of the maturity of the socialist country, was one of the first to adopt jet airliners. In June 1956, Aeroflot's Tupolev Tu-104 made its first appearance at Ruzyně Airport in Prague during a demonstration flight to several socialist countries. At the end of the same year, ČSA decided to buy three of these aircraft in order to modernise its fleet. The first Tu-104 in ČSA colours (OK-LDA) landed in Prague on 2 November 1957. Its first commercial flight took off on 9 December, serving the Prague to Moscow route. In August 1958, with the delivery of more Tu-104s, the type was also used on the Prague to Cairo route, and a year later, it operated a service to Bombay. Later on, the type would be used on the first ČSA route to the Far East, serving Jakarta via Cairo, Bombay, Rangoon and Phnom Penh. ČSA would operate a total of six Tu-104s, seating 80 passengers. After years of stagnation, there came a significant development in ČSA's international network. As well as the above mentioned route to the Far East, the airline added Amsterdam, Brussels, London and Tirana to its network.

While ČSA was expanding its activities, its Svitlet branch became loss-making. Therefore, it was decided to reduce the number of aircraft in that fleet and to modernise the remaining fleet. The Let L-200 Morava was selected to replace the old Aero 45s, and the first ten Moravas would enter the fleet in mid-January 1961.

In 1960, ČSA introduced the Ilyushin Il-18 four-engined turboprop. The first two (OK-NAA and OK-NAB) touched down in Prague on 8 January, and one of them made the inaugural flight on the Prague–Bratislava route on 29 January. Two days later, the aircraft made its first intercontinental flight, linking Prague with Conakry via Zürich, Rabat and Dakar. In general, the Il-18 would be used on domestic routes, but it could also be seen at European airports, and in the Middle East, the Il-18 operated the Prague–Athens–Damascus–Baghdad route. The first ČSA flight to Bamako in Mali was also operated by an Il-18 on 25 February 1961. That year, the service to Mumbai was extended by adding Colombo to the route map. Strangely enough, although ČSA was only buying Soviet-built aircraft, two Bristol 175 Britannias, OK-MBA and OK-MBB, joined the fleet. These were on loan from Cubana and would be used on a regular service to the Cuban capital of Havana. The first of these aircraft would remain in service till May 1964, whereas the second one was retired in May 1969.

While ČSA was modernising its fleet, Agrolet also obtained new aircraft. Two Mil Mi-1 and two Mil Mi-4 helicopters joined the fleet, and this unit's range of activities expanded to include construction and assembly, geological surveying and film making, as well as supplying alpine chalets. In 1962, ČSA started up a direct Prague–Dakar service and added Marseille, Ankara and Beirut to the network. Having

Shortly after the communist coup, the Soviet Union delivered a series of Ilyushin Il-12 aircraft. (Alan Bushell)

commenced the connection with Havana, its Bristol Britannia would later be used on flights to Mexico City and Merida. In 1963, Tehran was added to the rapidly expanding ČSA timetable.

By 1961, it had become clear that Ruzyně Airport had to be expanded, taking into account the growth of ČSA's traffic. Construction on the new North area (now Terminal 1) started in 1964. That year, ČSA carried more than 1 million passengers for the first time. Regular flights to Kabul, Afghanistan, were inaugurated and Tupolev Tu-124 jets were added to the fleet. These were smaller than the Tu-104 and could seat 56 passengers. By 1967, ČSA was one of the 34 airlines in the world to carry more than 1 million passengers. The airline ranked 29th in the world and was in the top ten among European countries.

Besides the Il-12, the Soviet Union also delivered Lisunov Li-2 aircraft. (Prague Ruzyně Airport archive, public domain)

ČSA also operated a fleet of Ilyushin Il-14 aircraft. Most of them were built under licence by Avia in Czechoslovakia. (Alan Bushell)

This Avia 14 is otherwise an Ilyushin Il-14, built under licence by Avia. (Peter Keating collection via Alan Bushell)

The first Tupolev Tu-104 in ČSA colours arrived in Prague in November 1957. (Thijs Postma)

A ČSA Tupolev Tu-104. (Peter Keating collection via Alan Bushell)

Svitlet used a fleet of Aero-45 aircraft. (FORTEPAN / Budapest Főváros Levéltára Creative Commons Attribution-Share Alike 3.0 Unported, commons.wikimedia.org/wiki/File:Aero_Ae-45._-_Fortepan_104281.jpg)

ČSA bought ten Moravas for its Svitlet subsidiary. (Fortepan, public domain)

Although ČSA operated mainly Soviet-made aircraft, it also used two Bristol Britannias on loan from Cubana. (Richard Goring, Creative Commons Attribution-Share Alike 2.0 Generic, commons.wikimedia.org/wiki/File:Bristol_175_Britannia_318_OK-MBB,_Ceskoslovenske_Aerolinie_(ČSA),_Southend,_UK,_02_Sep_1966_(9040223443).jpg)

Besides the Tupolev Tu-104, ČSA also used the smaller Tu-124.(Jack de Nijs for Anefo, Nationaal Archief, public domain, Creative Commons CC0 1.0 Universal Public Domain Dedication, commons.wikimedia.org/wiki/File:Opdracht_Telegraaf_Toepoelov_op_Schiphol,_Bestanddeelnr_917-2177.jpg)

This Tupolev Tu-124 is being prepared for its next flight. (Alan Bushell)

The Ilyushin Il-18 was mainly used on domestic routes, but could also be seen at European airports. (Alan Bushell)

Arrival of a ČSA Ilyushin Il-18. (ČSA)

Above: ČSA's subsidiary Agrolet used the L-60B Brigadyr for agricultural work. (ČSA)

Right: Agrolet also used a series of helicopters to perform work in the sectors of construction and surveillance. (Jozef Mols collection)

Chapter 6

The Prague Spring

From 1965, ČSA had been planning to modernise its ageing Soviet-made fleet. Having taken the Britannias on loan from Cubana, the airline was once again considering the purchase of British-made aircraft such as the Vickers Super VC10 for long-distance flights, and the de Havilland DH. 121 Trident plus BAC One-Eleven for medium-haul routes. ČSA also entered into negotiations with American companies like Boeing and Douglas about the possible purchase of Douglas DC-8 and Boeing 707 types. ČSA's management recognised that its Soviet-built aircraft operating international routes did not comply with ICAO regulations. The USSR constructed planes according to its own 'durability norms' and corresponding regulations, and did not pay much attention to the rest of the world. But as the purchase of Western aircraft types was out of the question for both financial and political reasons, ČSA was resigned to borrowing Ilyushin Il-62 aircraft from the USSR. On 2 May 1968, the first four-engined Il-62 was handed over to ČSA for trial operation. The following year, this type was put into regular service on routes to Africa, the Middle East and the Far East. In the meantime, the airline had started up further new international routes to Kiev (via Kosice), Algiers, Zagreb, Tunis, Freetown, Singapore and Istanbul. In 1968, the timetable was enriched once again with flights to Nicosia, Kuwait, Leningrad, Geneva and Marseille. By that time, the new improved Terminal 1 at Ruzyně Airport in Prague had been opened.

While ČSA was rapidly expanding its network, Czechoslovakians living under communism could enjoy newfound freedoms in a period known as the Prague Spring. New leader Alexander Dubček shook up the political establishment by implementing freedom of the press, freedom of speech and freedom of travel, along with economic reforms. These liberalisation efforts, which he called 'socialism with a human face', won popular support from his citizens. But at the same time, they alarmed other communist countries such as the Soviet Union, East Germany, Poland, Hungary and Bulgaria. Dubček made it clear he wanted to remain loyal to his 'master', the Soviet Union, and remain a member of the Warsaw Pact. But this was not enough for Moscow. On 20 August 1968, several hundred thousand Soviet, Polish, Hungarian and Bulgarian troops rolled into Czechoslovakia. East Germany did not participate in the invasion, because the image of Germans invading Czechoslovakia would be particularly unwelcome after Nazi Germany's invasion of the country only 30 years previously. There was little or no armed resistance, but protesters flooded the streets, confronting tanks with flowers, taking down street signs to confuse the soldiers and yelling: 'Ivan, go home'. Some 100 protesters were killed by the invading troops. Dubček was arrested and flown to Moscow. A few days later, he returned to Prague, informing his fellow citizens he had to take temporary measures that would limit democracy and freedom of opinion. In the West, there was little reaction to the Soviet invasion. The United States, heavily engaged in the Vietnam War, was not willing to hamper its ongoing arms-control negotiation with the Soviet Union[1]. As a result of the invasion, Prague Ruzyně Airport was taken over by the Soviet Air Force and ČSA had to suspend operations. After 14 days, the airline could resume flights, but it would take two more years before domestic services returned to a pre-invasion level, and a large loss of revenue resulted.

Notwithstanding tensions between the Warsaw Pact countries and the United States, the governments of Czechoslovakia and the USA signed an agreement on air transport on

2 February 1969. This allowed ČSA to start up regular transatlantic routes. New York and Montreal were the first destinations on the North American continent and these destinations were served with the Ilyushin Il-62. The first commercial flight took off from Prague in May 1970. Shortly afterwards, operations on the Prague–Luxembourg, Bratislava–Paris and Bratislava–Frankfurt routes were launched. In the same month, ČSA also launched its new long-haul route linking Prague with Kuala Lumpur, operated by Ilyushin Il-62s. In the meantime and as a result of the Constitutional Act of the Czechoslovak Federation, Czechoslovakia had been transformed into a federal state in 1968. This act stipulated the creation of two constituent republics, with separate government structures for the Czech Socialist Republic located in Prague, and those of the Slovak Socialist Republic situated in Bratislava. As a result, ČSA's subsidiary Agrolet became a separate company called Slov-Air, with its headquarters in Bratislava. A large part of ČSA's fleet of small aircraft, including Let L-200 Moravas and Aero Brigadýrs, passed to Slov-Air.

After the introduction of the Il-62 on ČSA's long-haul routes, it was time to look for new equipment for the medium-haul market segment. At the end of 1971, the first twin-engined Tupolev Tu-134A aircraft with 76 seats joined the fleet. The type would be part of ČSA for 25 years. When further units arrived, they would be used on busy domestic routes, as well as medium-haul routes across Europe and North Africa. The Tu-134 would make its first commercial flight in early December 1971 on the Prague–Bratislava route. In the meantime, the airline had added Tripoli to its route network, followed by a service to Madrid via Geneva and Marseille. And for the first time, ČSA also went beyond the Arctic Circle by offering a Prague–Helsinki–Rovaniemi flight. In 1973, when the airline marked its half-century of existence, it offered connections to 49 destinations abroad and 10 in Czechoslovakia[2].

ČSA was happy to borrow Ilyushin Il-62 aircraft from Aeroflot, as it was not possible to buy American-made equipment. (Alan Bushell)

Ilyushin Il-62 CCCP-86675 was also on loan from Aeroflot and would be returned to the USSR in 1974. (Alan Bushell)

After borrowing Soviet Il-62s for trial operations, ČSA would buy a series of this type, which were registered in Czechoslovakia. (Alan Bushell)

The Tupolev Tu-134A joined the fleet in 1971. (Jozef Mols)

The Tu-134A would become the backbone of ČSA's medium-haul fleet. (Jozef Mols)

In 1968, ČSA celebrated its 45th birthday. (Alan Bushell)

Chapter 7

End of an Era

Over the past years, ČSA had introduced new Soviet-made aircraft for medium and long haul lights. In April 1974, the last Tu-104A in its fleet left the airline after flying the Prague–Ostrava–Prague route for the final time. That same year, the first Yakovlev Yak-40 jet entered the fleet, chosen as a replacement for the Ilyushin Il-14. ČSA first leased two Yaks for trial operations and then, over the course of two years, amassed 17 of these small passenger jets. These jets were able to transport 32 passengers, though some were the 'K'-version, equipped with large cargo doors, and were used to transport both cargo and people. In January 1975, ČSA could announce that it carried more than one million passengers on domestic routes for the first time in its history[1]. 1975 also saw the airline start to use the SITA Gabriel automated reservation system.

In early 1976, ČSA took over the small transport service of Slov-Air, including aircraft, crew and the route network. Let L-410A Turbolet aircraft thus joined the fleet. These aircraft, produced by Let Kunovice, were equipped for 16 passengers and powered by two Pratt & Whitney of Canada PWC PT6A-27 engines. They would be used on domestic routes till 1981, when they were put up for sale. In 1977, the last Avia Av-14 made its last flight on the Kosice–Bratislava–Brno–Prague route, marking this type's final appearance with ČSA after 20 years of service.

The airline now further expanded its network by adding a Prague–Barcelona route in 1977 and Prague–Athens–Larnaca, Bratislava–Warsaw and Bratislava–Leningrad routes in 1978. As with many other airlines around the world, however, ČSA was hit by the oil crisis, which caused a huge leap in fuel prices and a worsening global economic situation. The airline had to adopt austerity measures, removing uneconomical aircraft from the fleet and grounding the Let L-410As and Yak-40s. Certain routes were cancelled to reduce operational costs. Flights to Dakar, Casablanca, Rabat, Marseille and Jakarta were halted altogether, while the network of domestic flights was reduced. Only the basic routes between Prague, Ostrava, Košice, Poprad and Sliač remained in operation. In order to offset increasing fuel prices, ČSA introduced the first modernised and more fuel-efficient Ilyushin Il-62M. This type would inaugurate the first new route after the oil crisis, when it was used on a service from Prague to Hanoi via Yerevan and Tashkent. By 1982, ČSA was operating services on six domestic routes and 44 destinations abroad. In 1983, an additional route to Dubai was introduced and, during the summer, a seasonal route to Malta was opened. In 1984, a new seasonal service to Lisbon began. For the first time, ČSA also introduced Business Class on board its aircraft.

Due to the oil crisis that begin in April 1979, and the resulting austerity measures, ČSA reduced its operations with the result that passenger numbers declined by 40 per cent when compared to the pre-crisis year of 1979[2]. Nevertheless, the airline was doing better than many other IATA members. In 1985, ČSA reported an increase in passenger kilometres over the previous year of some 9.1 per cent, whereas for IATA, the average was only 5.9 per cent. By that time, ČSA also decided to lease government-owned Tupolev Tu-154s and ordered the same type of aircraft from the manufacturer. When these new aircraft entered the fleet, the tail logo was changed, and the 'OK JET' inscription on rudders was gradually replaced by 'OK ČSA'. OK-SCA was ČSA's first new Tupolev Tu-154M and entered the fleet in 1988. Later on, six more would arrive in Prague. In the meantime, new services to Sochi, Simferopol and Tbilisi were launched, together with a seasonal service to Split, starting in June 1986.

While the airline had been challenged by the oil crisis, the aviation industry had also undergone changes. At the same time, the populations of the socialist countries started to see that the socialist camp was in a very bad state, no longer the 'workers' paradise' that the governments wanted them to believe. In many boardrooms, including that of ČSA, managers were eyeing economic freedoms in the West. In Czechoslovakia, a market economy had emerged and both the country and ČSA began to lean more towards the West, even dropping some routes to 'friendly' socialist countries. When the management started planning its fleet renewal, they considered the advantages and disadvantages of Western aircraft and compared them with the offerings from Soviet manufacturers. New Soviet-built aircraft such as the Ilyushin Il-86 and later Il-96 were considered, but it became clear that delivery times were unpredictable. Western manufacturers could supply good aircraft on short notice. Of course, the price of such aircraft would be much higher than Soviet-built competitors; nevertheless, ČSA embarked tentatively upon initial talks with Airbus Industries. As these progressed, ČSA introduced its first Tu-154M on a Prague–London route. For the 1988/89 winter flight schedule, Bangkok appeared as a stopover on the new Prague–Singapore route, and, in early 1989, ČSA resumed flights between Prague and Vienna. During the Paris Air Show the same year, it was announced that ČSA and Airbus Industries had signed an agreement relating to the delivery of two Airbus A310-300 aircraft. These would be the first Western-made aircraft to be ordered by the Czechoslovak airline after the war. A few days later, by memorandum of association issued by the decision of the Minister of Transport and Communications of the Czechoslovak Socialist Republic, ČSA was established as a state enterprise on 1 July 1989.

The Yakovlev Yak-40 replaced the old Ilyushin Il-14. (Alan Bushell)

The Yakovlev Yak-40 had a rear door under the tail; in combination with the front passenger door, it allowed for quick boarding. (Alan Bushell)

As new jets entered the fleet, the tail logo on the aircraft was changed from OK JET to OK ČSA. (Alan Bushell)

ČSA introduced the more fuel-efficient Ilyushin Il-62M as a result of the oil crisis. (Jozef Mols)

The Tupolev Tu-154 was the most modern Soviet-made jet in the fleet. This one is wearing the new paint scheme. (Jozef Mols)

A Tupolev Tu-154, still wearing the old colour scheme but with the new OK ČSA tail logo. (Alan Bushell)

ČSA took over the small aircraft operations of Slov-Air, including the fleet of Let L-410 Turbolet aircraft. (Piergiuliano Chesi, Creative Commons Attribution 3.0 Unported, commons.wikimedia.org/wiki/File:Let_L-410_Turbolet_OK-DKC.jpg)

A ČSA Let L-410 Turbolet in the snow. (Thijs Postma)

Chapter 8

The Velvet Revolution

During the 1980s, people in the socialist countries started to compare their living conditions with those experienced in the West. Freedom of speech and freedom of the press were unheard of in the East, and travel outside the socialist bloc was restricted to a lucky few. People faced persecution by the authorities; writers or filmmakers could have their books or films banned for a negative attitude towards the socialist regime. Discontent with living standards and economic inadequacy gave way to popular support for economic reform and citizens began to challenge the system. By 1989, people who had been complacent were willing to openly express their discontent with the regime. Reform-minded attitudes were represented by the many individuals who signed a petition that circulated in the summer of 1989, calling for the end of censorship and the beginning of fundamental political reforms. The same developments could be observed in neighbouring countries including East Germany, whose citizens had occupied the West German embassy in Prague and demanded admission to West Germany. On 9 November, the Berlin Wall fell. On the eve of International Students' Day (the 50th anniversary of Sonderaktion Prag, the 1939 storming of Prague universities by the Nazis), Slovak high school and university students organised a peaceful demonstration in the centre of Bratislava. On 18 November, two students visited Prime Minister Ladislav Adamec to explain their demands. At the same time, students and actors of the many theatres in Czechoslovakia went on strike. A few days later, uncensored live reports of demonstrations in the country could be seen on national TV. On 24 November, the entire Presidium of the Communist Party resigned. Karel Urbánek, a more moderate communist, was named General Secretary of the party. By that time, more than 800,000 people were demonstrating in the streets of Prague. On 28 November, the Federal Assembly deleted the provision in the constitution referring to the 'leading role' of the Communist Party, officially ending communist rule in Czechoslovakia. On 10 December, President Gustáv Husák swore in the first government in 41 years that was not dominated by the Communist Party. On 29 December, after the resignation of Husák, well-known dissident Václav Havel became president[1].

Obviously, these events in had significant implications for the national airline. As travel was no longer restricted to fellow socialist countries, people now had the possibility to voyage further afield, and therefore the airline had to expand its network. At the same time, the start of a free market economy also made it possible for ČSA to look abroad when it wanted to replace older Soviet-made aircraft with more modern Western equipment. On 31 December 1989, the era of the ageing Ilyushin Il-18 in the service of ČSA came to an end. The last flight of this type on a scheduled service was operated by OK-VAF on the Prague–Bratislava–Leningrad route. In 1991, ČSA purchased its first two Airbus A310-300s to replace the two earlier models of the same type that had been leased. OK-WAA arrived in Prague on 14 February 1991 and was christened *Praha*. The second one (OK-WAB) joined the fleet on 12 March 1991 and was christened *Bratislava*. Both aircraft were used on long-haul routes[2]. In 1990, the airline had started up a regular service linking Prague with Hamburg, but, as a result of the political changes in the country, ČSA's regular services to Hanoi and Havana were simultaneously ended. Additionally, relations between Czechoslovakia and Israel were normalised, with ČSA now able to commence regular flights to Tel Aviv.

Another important event would further influence ČSA's activities. In 1990, the Federal Assembly approved an amendment to the Civil Aviation Act, abolishing the state monopoly over aviation and allowing private carriers to be established. The state airports were also separated from the state enterprise ČSA, and the new 'Ceska Sprava Letist' (Czech Airport Management or CSL) was subsequently established[3]. This would open the door to domestic and international competitors to challenge ČSA. However, only a handful of air taxi operators set up office in the first years after the liberalisation.

In January 1992, ČSA signed an agreement with ATR Aircraft for the delivery of four ATR-72s to be used on domestic and European routes. The first of them, OK-XFA, was delivered on 19 April 1992. Two years later, the airline received two smaller ATR-42s. Although successful, the capacity of the new aircraft could not be fully exploited on all services. Therefore, in order to make the operation more economical, Let-410 Turbolets, rented from the governmental squadron, would replace the ATRs on flights from Prague to Vienna. After the arrival of the ATRs, ČSA decided to also procure new Boeing 737-500 aircraft. The first of these, OK-XGA, joined the fleet in July. The Boeings or 'Bulici' (steers) as the ČSA staff fondly and affectionately referred to them, were the only American-manufactured jet aircraft in the company's history. They were very popular and reliable and would form the backbone of ČSA's fleet for well over 20 years. Over the years, ČSA would use a total of 30 737s (15 x 737-500s and 15 x 737-400s). However, with the aim of standardising the fleet, a decision was made in 2004 to phase out Boeings and to replace them with Airbuses[4]. In the meantime, the airline had added several new destinations to its network, including Chicago, Bahrain, Düsseldorf, Manchester, Toronto and Riga.

Fully in line with the free market policy adopted by the Czechoslovak government, ČSA began to set up co-operation with other airlines. A first initiative was a joint venture between ČSA and Air France. In 1992, Air France and the European Bank for Reconstruction and Development each acquired 19.1 per cent of ČSA shares. Other shareholders were the National Property Fund (49.3 per cent), Czech insurance company Česká pojišťovna (4.5 per cent), and the city of Prague (3.5 per cent), with the remaining shares in the hands of the cities of Bratislava, Košice and Poprad. The joint venture started operating in June 1992. At first, it seemed very promising as Prague is located in the heart of Europe, and as such could become an important crossroads for intra-European aviation. Unfortunately, the results did not confirm this optimism. ČSA ran into financial difficulties, which worsened in 1993. Even before entering the joint venture, Air France had stated that ČSA was badly managed and heavily burdened by expensive lease contracts. The French partner in the venture had its own problems, such as staff strikes and the fact that the airline could only survive thanks to government subsidies. Worldwide, many carriers were facing difficulties at this point in time. Pan American Airways, Eastern Airlines and British Caledonian even declared bankruptcy while other major carriers could only survive with government help. As a result of the difficulties experienced by ČSA, the services from Bratislava to Moscow, Chicago, New York and Montreal ceased. Further to the problems faced by the joint venture, Air France contemplated the possibility of withdrawing from the joint contract. During talks in Paris in 1994, a solution was found. Representatives of the Czech Ministry of Transport and Konsolidacni Banka negotiated a deal with representatives of Air France to allow the French carrier to exit from the joint venture without losing money. Ultimately, Konsolidacni Banka would take over Air France's portion of the deal, but it remained clear that ČSA would have to find a new strategic partner.

While ČSA was trying to solve its economic problems, political issues were raising their head. The 1968 Constitutional Law of Federation had created a federal structure, comprising a Czech Socialist Republic and a Slovak Socialist Republic under the umbrella of the Czechoslovak Socialist Republic. Despite being a Slovak himself, Gustáv Husák had concentrated most political control under Prague, an approach that encouraged the growth of Slovak separatism after the fall of communism. In 1991, the Czech Republic's GDP per capita was some 20 per cent higher than Slovakia's. Transfer payments from the Czech budget to Slovakia, which had been the rule in the past, were stopped in 1991. Though many Czechs and Slovaks desired the continued existence of a federal Czechoslovakia, some major Slovak parties advocated a looser form of co-existence or even complete independence. On 17 June 1992, the Slovak parliament adopted the declaration of independence of the Slovak nation. Six days later, at a meeting in Bratislava, it was agreed to divide Czechoslovakia into two separate states. But in contrast with Yugoslavia, where a violent break-up of the country had taken place, Czech and Slovak politicians wanted a peaceful division of the country. On 13 November, the division of property between the Czech lands and Slovakia was settled. As the partition occurred without violence, it was called the Velvet Divorce, in reference to the Velvet Revolution. Of course, federal assets had to be divided in a ratio of two to one, the approximate ratio between the Czech and Slovak population in the former Czechoslovakia. This included the airline infrastructure[5].

After 1993, the newly independent Slovakia found itself without a transport company; even in the past, the network of routes hadn't directly connected this region with the rest of the world. All direct flights from Bratislava to the outside world had been operated by ČSA, which was now a purely Czech company. Therefore, in 1995, Slovak Airlines was established, starting operations in 1998[6].

ČSA also had to adapt to the new reality. In 1992, ČSA had been transformed into a joint stock company when it entered the joint venture with Air France. Now, after the Velvet Divorce, the airline had to rationalise its name. Czechoslovak Airlines would become Czech Airlines, but the well-known abbreviation 'ČSA' was retained, as was the aircraft nationality mark 'OK'.

Right: The Airbus A310 was the first Western jet to join the ČSA fleet. (Aero Icarus, commons.wikimedia.org/wiki/Category:OKCC BY-SA 2.0-WAA_(aircraft)#/media/File:ČSA_Czech_Airlines_Airbus_A310-304;_OK-WAA@PRG,_March_1993_(5682509273).jpg)

Below: The Airbus A310-300 would remain the backbone of the long-haul fleet for a long time. This one carries the 80th-anniversary logo. (Jozef Mols)

The ATR-72 aircraft joined the fleet in 1992. (Jozef Mols)

Later on, the smaller ATR-42 was introduced on some regional lines. (ATR)

The Boeing 737 was the only American jet to enter the ČSA fleet. This is a 737-500, seen at Prague Airport. (Jozef Mols)

The 737 would remain in service for nearly 20 years. (Alan Bushell)

Slovenske Airolinie, which came into being after the division of Czechoslovakia, also used the Tupolev Tu-154. (Jozef Mols)

The Slovak flag carrier also used the Boeing 737, just like ČSA. (Jozef Mols)

Chapter 9

The New Millennium

Following 25 years of service in the ČSA fleet, the last Ilyushin Il-62 (OK-OBL) was retired after a flight from Brussels to Prague. In early 1997, the last Tupolev Tu-134 (OK-HFL) also departed, its last flight being from Prague to Belgrade. By that time, most of the older Soviet-era aircraft had either been sold to other airlines or retired. Some, however, were kept in reserve, having been replaced by Western models such as the Airbus A310 and Boeing 737-500. In March 1995, the first Boeing 737-400, OK-WGG, entered the fleet, followed a few days later by a second example, OK-WGF. ATR-42-300 aircraft, designed for shorter routes, were introduced for domestic services and nearby foreign destinations such as Poprad, Košice, Vienna, Munich, Berlin and Copenhagen. Of course, the introduction of the Boeing jets required an update of the training facilities. In June 2000, ČSA therefore opened a new training centre with Boeing 400/500 flight simulators.

After the co-operation with Air France ended, ČSA looked for other strategic partners. On 12 February 1996, an agreement with Continental Airlines was announced. This made it possible for ČSA to increase the number of flights to New York to seven per week in the summer season of 1996, connecting with 18 major US destinations served by Continental. This co-operation would also bring benefits to the members of ČSA's OK Plus incentive programme. Later, this frequent flyer programme was linked to Continental's 'One Pass'. When ČSA published its yearly report, it could announce the airline had returned to profitability. The profit amounted to some 244,000,000 Czech crowns (£ 7.9m), according to international accounting standards. The carrier had enjoyed an increase of 15 per cent in passenger numbers, flying to 56 destinations on four continents aboard 277 weekly flights.

As did many other airlines, ČSA restricted smoking on board its aircraft (on certain routes) in 1995. Smoking became prohibited on all flights in 1998, at which time it was also decided to stand down the remaining Tupolev Tu-154 jets from regular scheduled services, operating them only on charter flights in future. The last aircraft of this type, OK-UCE, was withdrawn in early 2000 after a charter flight between Prague and Istanbul. In a further expansion of the route network, new services to Bologna and Oslo were added in March 1998, followed by Nice and Amman a month later. The flights to the Norwegian capital were operated in co-operation with Braathens SAFE, ČSA passengers thus being able to make connections with 25 other destinations. Then, in early 1999, ČSA started flights to Dublin and Gothenburg.

After the changes to the Civil Aviation Act in 1990, new airlines would enter the scene. DSA had been incorporated in 1993, but, as this company specialised in medical services and helicopter flights, it was never a direct competitor to ČSA. Bemo Air started up as a cargo company for parcel post, but its bankruptcy in 1996 saw Egretta BMI formed from its remains. With its Ilyushin Il-62, Egretta BMI offered passenger charter flights from Prague Airport, but went bankrupt in turn a few months later, in October 1997.

Air Ostrava spol s.r.o was another Czech airline, founded on 1 January 1994 by Vitovice under the name Air Vitkovice spol s.r.o. The company took over aircraft from Air Vitkovice, which had been established in 1977 as a part of Vitkovice Iron Works. After 1989, it briefly operated regular passenger and cargo transport. Soon, the company was sold to JOB Air and on 19 May 1989, the name was changed to Air Ostrava Spol SRO and the headquarters transferred from Ostrava to Mošnov. In May 1995, the Chemapol Group became the owner of the airline, starting flights on the Ostrava–Prague route with Let L-410s in co-operation with ČSA. Later on, new aircraft were leased and used for flights from Ostrava to

Verona, Amsterdam and Nuremberg. In 2000, Air Ostrava ceased operations and declared bankruptcy without ever having been a serious competitor to ČSA[1].

Silver Air SRO was founded in 1995, operating a single Boeing 727-200 in Vietnam for a short period. With its fleet of Let L-410 Turbolet aircraft, the airline would then focus on passenger and cargo flights within Europe. The customers included global logistics companies such as DHL and TNT as well as the Czech Post. Although Silver Air is a Czech company, its passenger services are based at Marina di Campo Airport (Elba) in Italy, from where regular services to Bologna, Florence, Milan and Pisa are operated. Freight flights are exclusively operated in Romania[2].

Fisher Air became, in fact, the first solid competitor to ČSA. The new airline was incorporated by the K&K Capital Group in 1996 and, from its base in Prague, started operating a series of charter flights for tour operator Fisher, which belonged to the same financial group. The three Fisher Air Boeing 737-300s could soon be seen at more than 30 European destinations, as well as in North Africa. Although successful in the first years of operation, the airline went bankrupt in 2005 after it had been rebranded as Charter Air.

In an effort to tackle competition, ČSA decided to start selling tickets directly to the public beginning in September 2000, though sales through travel agents and other ticket offices continued. The four last remaining Tu-154s, which by now were only used on charter operations, were sold to Bulgaria's Hemus Air. In the first half of 2000, ČSA reported a record surplus of some 205m Czech crowns (£7.2m), thanks to the ever-growing demand for air transportation. The airline transported 1,105,847 passengers during the same period, which meant an increase of 22.8 per cent on the same period in 1999. The same period also showed an increase in cargo volume transported by ČSA, which was up 36.4 per cent compared with the same period in the previous year.

Most importantly, ČSA started negotiations on joining the new SkyTeam alliance. Original partners in the group included the Wings Group (KLM, Alitalia, Northwest Airlines and Continental) which, however, ceased to exist after the disruption of relations between KLM and Alitalia. At the same time, ČSA was also considering joining the emerging group with the working name of Global Alliance. This included Air France and Delta Airlines, and ČSA had the opportunity of becoming one of the founding members. Other carriers were to be Korean Air and Aeromexico. It was thought that Air France would return to a

Silver Air, although a Czech company, only operated outside the country. (Maarten Visser, CC BY-SA 2.0, en.wikipedia.org/wiki/Silver_Air_(Czech_Republic)#/media/File:OK-SLD_L-410_Silver_Air_(6157959575)_(2).jpg)

partnership with ČSA after six years, but this was now a completely different airline than the one that had left ČSA previously. It had gone through privatisation and had resolved its problems with the trade unions.

Ultimately, ČSA decided to continue negotiations with Skyteam. At that time, several commissions were already working on media campaigns, so ČSA could no longer be mentioned in the press communications and could not be considered as a founding member of the alliance. But to ČSA, this was not of great importance. The statute of the alliance does not distinguish between founding members and other members that joined later on.

Bemo Air started up as a parcel company but soon obtained an Ilyushin Il-62, which was used for passenger and cargo transport. (Jozef Mols collection)

When Bemo Air encountered financial problems, Egretta BMI was set up out of its remains. (Jozef Mols collection)

Air Ostrava initiated passenger flights between Ostrava and Prague with a fleet of mainly Saab 340s. (Jozef Mols collection)

This Air Ostrava Saab 340 is painted in the standard paint scheme of the airline. (Jozef Mols collection)

This British Aerospace Jetstream 31 served in the Air Ostrava fleet from 1995 till 1997. (Jozef Mols collection)

This Fokker 28 Fellowship was only used during a very short period in 1996. (Jozef Mols collection)

Fischer Air offered passenger charter flights with a fleet of three Boeing 737-300s. (Jozef Mols collection)

Travel Service would, in the long run, be the only serious competitor to ČSA among the many Czech airlines. (Jozef Mols collection)

ČSA also added the Boeing 737-400 to its fleet. (Aero Icarus, Creative Commons Attribution-Share Alike 2.0 Generic, commons.wikimedia.org/wiki/File:145gi_-_ČSA_Czech_Airlines_Boeing_737-45S,_OK-DGM@CDG,11.08.2001_-_Flickr_-_Aero_Icarus.jpg)

Chapter 10

SkyTeam

Czech Airlines joined the SkyTeam alliance in March 2001. This step was to be expected, as Eastern European airlines had already had to adapt from Soviet-era practices to the disciplines of the Western market economy. ČSA itself had to learn quickly how to survive in such a competitive environment, and time was running out as the Czech Republic, together with seven other Eastern European countries, wanted to join the European Common Aviation Area in 2004[1]. Prime Minister Václav Klaus had made it clear that if ČSA was not able to survive on its own, the airline would disappear. This time, the government was not willing to help, as it had no doubts that many other carriers would serve Prague, and they didn't care whether this was ČSA or another airline[2]. ČSA thus had to adapt on its own. This was a time after the Gulf War when airlines around the world were receiving subsidies, but ČSA received nothing. ČSA had, just like many other European carriers, sought an alliance in the West, bringing in Air France with a minority stake. However, just as with other carriers, such a deal proved unsuccessful. Therefore, ČSA sought co-operation with a larger alliance.

ČSA talked to three major alliances before choosing Skyteam, fearing that if it did not join one of them, Hungarian flag carrier Malév might pick up the post. Of course, it was surprising that the Oneworld alliance had not shown more interest in Malév, given the fact that the Polish carrier LOT had joined the Star Alliance, leaving Oneworld as the only major alliance without a base in Eastern Europe[3]. When ČSA started talks with Lufthansa (Star Alliance) and British Airways (Oneworld), these airlines replied that they were not really interested, as their interest was mostly centred on picking up feeder traffic. Skyteam, on the other hand, was a brand new alliance that offered more opportunities for ČSA than joining one already established. Among other advantages, it would offer ČSA an exclusive position in Central and Eastern Europe[4]. ČSA already had a presence in North America, with flights to Toronto and Montreal (tapping the Eastern European diaspora market) and a summer service to New York-Newark, as well as a year-round flight to New York–JFK. Furthermore, the Czech Republic had signed an open skies agreement with the USA. Therefore, by joining Skyteam, ČSA could further build on its North American network. At the same time, ČSA was developing a role for Prague within Skyteam as a hub for Eastern Europe, while hoping to enlarge its presence in Asia with SkyTeam partner Korean Air. In the latter case, ČSA did not have aircraft able to fly the Prague–Seoul route, so this plan had to wait until around 2005, when Airbus A310s were to be replaced by either Airbus A330s or Boeing 767s. For the time being, Korean Air started up a regular flight from Seoul to Prague with Airbus A330 and Boeing 747 equipment in 2005. This flight was offered as a code-share operation between ČSA and Korean Air. Shortly after ČSA's entry into Skyteam, the airline signed a code-share agreement with Delta Airlines and it also became a member of Skyteam Cargo. To that end, construction of a brand new cargo terminal at Prague Airport commenced. The terminal became operational on 12 January 2004.

In 1999, the year ČSA started talks with partners in the SkyTeam Alliance, the airline had transported more than two million passengers with a fleet of 28 aircraft and had generated a net profit of US$2.8m. (£2.2m)[5]. The decision to join the alliance brought the total number of SkyTeam members to five, including founding members Delta and Air France, as well as Aeromexico and Korean Air.

Following its entrance into the alliance, ČSA started to rapidly expand its international network. In March 2001, Vilnius, Birmingham and Ljubljana were added to the timetable. Flights to Thessaloniki started in April. A year later, Cologne/Bonn and Venice were added. In 2004, the airline was offering connections to 75 destinations in 44 countries worldwide. The fleet had grown to 45 planes, and ČSA entered a completely new market when the Czech Republic joined the European Union. For the first time in its history, the airline could offer a connection fully outside the Czech Republic, flying the Marseille–Barcelona route. Cork, Edinburgh and Tallinn were added in April 2005. Long-haul operations also expanded with seasonal flights to Kuwait (June 2002) and regular lines to Colombo (October 2002).

As a consequence of all this new work, ČSA expanded its fleet. In October 2004, the airline placed an order for 12 new Airbus A320 and A319 aircraft. The first A320, OK-GEA, arrived in Prague on 17 March 2005, followed by a second example ten days later. The first A321, OK-CED, was delivered on 1 May of that year, with the second, OK-CEC, on 30 May. To cover the gap between the signing of the purchase contract and the delivery of the new aircraft from the factory, ČSA had bought or leased several other Airbus aircraft of the same family. At this point, ČSA had started seasonal charter flights to the resort of Varadero in Cuba, as well as flights to Fortaleza (Brazil) and Margarita Island (Venezuela). In order to facilitate access to Prague Airport, ČSA signed a code-share agreement with Czech Railways, which guaranteed fast rail transport with the Pendolino train from Ostrava, Olomouc and Pardubice to the international airport in Prague. However, competition also increased. Travel Service, which had operated seasonal charter flights for tour operators, launched its own low-cost brand, Smartwings, in 2004. For that purpose, Travel Service leased two Boeing 737-500s from Lufthansa, which were primarily intended for Smartwings' low-cost flights and therefore painted in the new Smartwings livery. EasyJet (through its Go acquisition) and BMIbaby had already entered the Czech market, and ČSA itself had also considered operating low-cost flights. However, it was decided not to follow that road, as it would have been necessary to lower service quality. On the Prague–London route, for example, ČSA's biggest competitor was not a low-cost carrier, but British Airways, which timed its flights to Prague to depart London Heathrow just minutes before the ČSA flight on the same route. This had a greater impact on ČSA's yields than the low-cost sector.

The fact that the Czech Republic had joined the European Union not only offered advantages to ČSA, but also caused some problems. Average salary levels in the Czech Republic had been much lower than in the EU, making it possible to compete with foreign carriers prior to membership. Czechs, just like all airline employees, dreamt about dramatic increases in salary levels once the republic became a part of the European Union, so ČSA had to negotiate a new collective wage deal, for which the demands of the unions were very high.

At the beginning of 2006, ČSA presented its audited results for the year 2005. Even though it had transported more than five million passengers for the first time, it ended up with a loss of 496 million crowns (20.1m euros or £17.4m). Total operating revenues had risen by 12 per cent, but operating costs grew more quickly by 21.4 per cent, while oil prices had increased by 45 per cent. The cost of operational leases and increased wages also had a negative effect on the results. Even so, the airline had managed to increase its market share at Prague Airport from 44.8 per cent to 48.4 per cent.

For the period 2006–08, ČSA had to develop a new strategy, known as 'OK 06-08'. A new organisational plan aimed to bring the airline into profit by 2008, and one of its main points was to separate the marketing and sales division into two separate departments. Jaroslav Stepanek, who had been the executive director of sales, was appointed as the new temporary head of the sales division. Marie Macounova, who had been working in sales and marketing, became vice president of the new marketing and product development division. Marcela Hrda, who was previously vice president for marketing and sales, was moved to a different position within the airline while Jan Vana, executive director for strategic planning and development, left his position[6]. Besides the management shake-up, ČSA emphasised its intention to maintain the high quality of in-flight services. Indeed, in 2006 the airline had won the Best Airline in Eastern Europe award from the American magazine *Global Traveler*, and this for the second time in a row. A survey conducted by IATA showed that passenger satisfaction with Czech Airlines was among the highest in Europe. Furthermore, the airline was considering the introduction of new long-distance operations to India, China and Vietnam, plus some cost-saving measures and restructuring, including the sale of subsidiaries such as catering and duty-free shops. A reduction of staff by some ten per cent, mainly in administration, was also considered. As for the fleet, further expansion was not planned and the airline would return older leased aircraft to their owners.

In 2001, ČSA joined the SkyTeam Alliance. (Karelj, public domain, commons.wikimedia.org/wiki/File:Airbus_A319_Prague_airport_2015_1.jpg)

This Airbus A319, delivered in 2010, shows the paint scheme of the SkyTeam Alliance. (Raymond Zammit)

Some ATRs also received the new SkyTeam livery. (Jozef Mols collection)

When ČSA celebrated its 80th birthday in 2003, this Boeing 737 received a special livery. (ČSA archive)

This Airbus A321 was leased from GATX in 2005 after having served with Air France and Air Canada. The aircraft entered the fleet while ČSA was awaiting delivery of its own Airbus aircraft from the factory. (Jozef Mols)

An Airbus A321 is being prepared for its next flight at Prague Ruzyně Airport. (Rottweiler, public domain, commons.wikimedia.org/wiki/Category:Airbus_A321_of_Czech_Airlines_at_Prague_Ruzyn%C4%9B_Airport#/media/File:A321_CSA.jpg)

Chapter 11

Diamonds

Fully in line with the 'OK 06-08' restructuring plan, ČSA undertook a major rebranding exercise in 2007, in which the airline's logo was rejuvenated by Czech graphic artist Michal Kotyza. It took him six months of work to design a logo that would remove the post-communist image with which foreign clientele still identified Czech Airlines. The new logo was simultaneously intended to enable application accelerating to subsidiaries or individual products. The previous logo, made up of triangles, and launched in the early 1990s, were replaced by a visual resembling a diamond or, for some, a 'pick' as might be used to play a guitar. The traditional ČSA logo was incorporated into this red element and supplemented with 'Czech Airlines' to make its country clearer to foreign clients[1]. ČSA employees also received a new uniform.

A few months after the introduction of the new house style, ČSA took delivery of its first Airbus A319, OK-MEK. As the airline had ordered several of these modern jets, a new training centre was opened, featuring an Airbus A320 flight simulator. These were followed in the early days of 2008 by four more new A319s.

In June 2007, ČSA customers, departing from Prague, Paris and Amsterdam, could for the first time check-in online on the company's website. At the end of the year, ČSA won the prestigious Best Airline in Central Europe award in the Skytrax World Airline Awards. Skytrax, originally known as Inflight Research Services, is a United Kingdom-based consultancy headquartered in London; it runs an airline and airport review website.

Smartwings, the low-cost subsidiary of Travel Service (and ČSA's main Czech competitor), also underwent changes. It had carried about 2.2 million passengers that year. On 18 September 2007, Icelandair Group acquired a 50 per cent stake in the airline, plus options to purchase further shares to bring its holding up to 80 per cent by April 2008[2].

In the meantime, on the other side of the Atlantic Ocean, a storm front was brewing. The American financial crisis would soon become the most severe economic crisis since the Great Depression of 1929. Predatory lending in the form of subprime mortgages, the targeting of low-income homebuyers and excessive risk-taking by global financial institutions, together with a continuous build-up of toxic assets within banks would culminate in a 'perfect storm'. Whereas at first only the US economy seemed to be hit, soon it became clear that the globalisation of the financial system would spread the fall-out of the American housing bubble to financial institutions all over the world, including those of Europe. Economies worldwide slowed down during this period as credit tightened, and international trade declined, while unemployment soared.[3]

Before the crisis, the economies in industrial countries had been characterised by high production growth up until the beginning of 2008; this trend was dampened by the events in the US real estate markets in the middle of the year, leading first to a credit crunch and finally to the recession. This would, of course, also affect the aviation sector. While the first half of the year saw growth, the opposite was the case for the rest of 2008, when passenger numbers dropped drastically. In terms of global air traffic, 0.4 per cent fewer passengers were recorded. While demand went down, the number of passenger kilometres offered by airlines in comparison increased by 1.3 per cent, leading to lower occupancy rates. All world regions were differently affected. While air traffic shrank in Africa by four per cent, above average growth was observed in the Middle East (over seven per cent) and Latin America (over 10.2 per cent). Europe's growth of 3.7 per cent could be considered a moderate level. But not all European carriers could profit from this growth. As seats offered were continually adjusted to meet expectations, the full service network carriers slightly reduced their capacity offered by one per cent. Holiday/charter carriers reduced their supply by up to 25 per cent in response to the sales decline. Conversely, the low-cost carriers saw great expansion as crisis-induced price awareness led passengers away from the full-fare carriers and into the arms of the low-cost segment. These carriers would dominate the number of new routes opened, whereas many of the routes closed had been offered before by network airlines[4]. ČSA's competitor Smartwings, for example, saw its traffic rise from 2.2 million passengers in 2007 to 2.4 million a year later. And ČSA still made a profit in 2007 and 2008, despite the negative developments. It was only in 2009 that the airline would begin to suffer from the crisis. Its turnover diminished slightly, but cashflow was already declining considerably. Although ČSA's financial situation deteriorated as early as late 2008, the Czech authorities had reason to believe that significantly better results would be achieved in the 2009 summer season, when revenues in the airline industry commonly peak. Nevertheless, the results of the first half of 2009 showed a significant decline in average revenue. It became clear that the airline would no longer be able to run its business without immediate cost-cutting measures and financial assistance from external sources. As a result, the Board of Directors established a working group, instructing it to prepare a restructuring plan for the company[5].

As a further consequence, the Czech Ministry of Finance announced a tender for the purchase of the majority stake in Czech Airlines. Four bidders entered the competition; Air France-KLM, the Oden Group and Darofan of the Aeroflot Group (which had recently become a member of the Skyteam Alliance), as well as a consortium of the Unimex Group and Travel Service[6]. However, European regulations did not allow Aeroflot to buy more than 49 per cent of ČSA. Therefore, the Russians planned to enter a joint partnership with a Czech-owned company or legal entity for the second stage of the privatisation[7]. The Oden Group, on the other hand, was a well-respected real estate developer in Eastern Europe with main

This Airbus A319, delivered in 2007, received the revised 'diamond' logo. (Raymond Zammit)

offices in Prague. Unimex was a dominant business group in the Czech Republic. Ultimately, only the Unimex Group and the Travel Service consortium submitted a final bid, but the Czech government rejected the offers and halted the process of privatising Czech Airlines[8].

Notwithstanding the economic crisis, ČSA added several new destinations to its timetable, including Strasbourg in March 2008, Tbilisi and Rostov-on-Don in April of the same year, and Almaty in May. By the end of 2008, ČSA had transported a historic record number of passengers, more than 5.6 million. But, by adding new destinations and passenger kilometres to its network, its occupancy rate had dropped.

A ČSA Airbus A319, showing the new livery, on approach to Malta International Airport. (Raymond Zammit)

This Airbus A320 with its new diamond logo represents good publicity for Prague Airport. (Prague Ruzyně Airport)

This A319, which was delivered in 2008 and at first carried the 'diamond' logo, was repainted in City of Prague livery in 2014. (Dominik Czordas)

The ATR aircraft has also received the 'diamond' logo. (Lukáš Musil Creative Commons Attribution-Share Alike 4.0 International, commons.wikimedia.org/wiki/File:ATR_72,_Czech_Airlines.jpg)

An ATR-72 in the new livery on approach. (Lumikus1 Creative Commons Attribution-Share Alike 4.0 International, commons.wikimedia.org/wiki/File:ATR_72,_Czech_Airlines,_OK-GFO.jpg)

The older Boeing 737-500s also received the new logo. (Martin Vavřík, public domain, commons.wikimedia.org/wiki/Category:Boeing_737_of_Czech_Airlines_at_Prague_Ruzyn%C4%9B_Airport#/media/File:Czech_Airlines_B737-55S_(OK-CGK)_landing_at_Prague_Ruzyn%C4%9B_Airport.jpg

The Unimex Group and its subsidiary Travel Service made a bid to take over ČSA. (Jozef Mols)

Chapter 12

Korean Air Enters the Scene

After the Czech government had rejected the takeover bid by the Unimex Group and Travel Service, and had halted the process of privatising the airline, key questions remained over the future of the flag carrier. Could it remain a niche network carrier or would it have to become a regional feeder airline? The government decided that it would have to continue with restructuring. According to ČSA CEO Radomír Lašák, the airline needed to accelerate cost-cutting and take drastic action, including staff reductions, the cutting of routes and the disposal of aircraft in order to return to profitability in 2010. Three 737s could be returned to the lessors on expiry of their operating leases, while the route from Prague to New York was closed, SkyTeam partner Delta maintaining the service. ČSA insisted, however, that it would remain a long-haul carrier, with routes continuing to central Asian destinations, despite these routes being flown with narrow-body aircraft. A code-share with China Eastern on the Frankfurt–Shanghai route was planned to start in 2011.

As all of this was going on, the Czech pilots' union CZALPA wrote a letter to the Czech prime minister, criticising the airline's management and, in particular, its decision to cancel long-haul routes. ČSA simultaneously told the union that it wanted to make 860 redundancies at the airline, out of a total staff of 4,600. These would include 140 of the 560 pilots, and 240 cabin crew. Such a scheme, however, ran into opposition, so, in October, the company said it wanted to cut salaries, with the board promising to resign as soon as the union signed new collective agreements with cuts of 30 per cent to pilot salaries, a 15 per cent reduction in other salaries and a freeze on all other employee benefits until the end of 2010. When the deal was accepted, chairman Václav Novák, CEO Radomir Lasak and six other board members resigned. Miroslav Zámečník took over as chairman and Miroslav Dvorak, head of Prague Airport, became the carrier's new CEO. Soon afterwards, the chairman was replaced again, this time by Michal Majstrik, and the management board was cut from nine to five members.

In order to raise cash, ČSA decided to dispose of some of its non-core assets. The duty-free business, with 80 employees and annual revenue of more than £23m, was sold to the French retail and distribution group Lagadère Services. The biggest move, however, came when the airline sold its administrative building at Prague Airport for 607m Kc (£20.5m) to the Prague airport authority. The airline would thereafter lease back the building, putting the cash towards other areas. It was hoped that this capital would significantly strengthen the company, but the following years would be very challenging. In 2010–11, a new joint-stock company, Czech Aeroholding, was set up by the Czech government. Czech Airlines became a subsidiary of Czech Aeroholding, which also included Prague Airport (the operator of the airport), Czech Airlines Technics (a provider of services in technical maintenance) and Czech Airlines Handling.

Despite wrestling with financial problems, ČSA expanded its network again. On 24 April 2011, a new service from Prague to Donetsk was launched. Two months later, routes from Bratislava to

Amsterdam, Paris, Rome, Brussels, Barcelona and Larnaca were opened. And in September, regular flights from Prague to Abu Dhabi started. A joint co-operation with Etihad Airways was agreed for a long-haul service from Prague via Abu Dhabi to Southeast Asia and Africa and, in the other direction, Etihad Airways' clients could continue their journey from Prague on ČSA's network in Europe.

In December 2012, Czech Airlines resumed its long-haul flights with a new service to Seoul, in a code-share operation with Korean Air. ČSA believed that the future of the aviation business required connections to Asia and, in order to operate these flights, obtained a long-haul Airbus A330 on the basis of operative leasing from Korean Air. In Seoul, ČSA would offer, thanks to its co-operation with Korean Air, connections to Japan, China and the Pacific. In return, Prague would become a gateway for Asian passengers visiting Europe. Besides flights to Asia, the Airbus would also be used on routes to the Commonwealth of Independent States. New short-haul routes, including destinations such as Perm, Nice, Munich, Zürich and Florence were also considered. Brisbane, Singapore and Nairobi were included in the 2013 flight schedule, operated in co-operation with Etihad Airways. When the Airbus joined the fleet, the Boeing 737-500 jets were retired. The airline thus operated only two aircraft makes (Airbus and ATR).

While ČSA was expanding its network and restructuring its fleet, Czech finance minister Miroslav Kalousek announced that the government had approached some 50 airlines in the hopes of persuading them to take a strategic stake in ČSA. Only Korean and Qatar Airways expressed an interest, and, under EU rules, they would only be able to take a 49 per cent stake in the carrier if the airline wanted to retain its status as a European airline[1].

In 2013, Korean Air obtained a 44 per cent stake in ČSA. Furthermore, this airline exercised the option to purchase a further 34 per cent of the Czech carrier, on the condition that Korean Air would immediately sell the shares obtained via the option to Travel Service, which in this way would become a co-shareholder of Korean Air (44 per cent), the others being Czech Aeroholding (19.74 per cent) and Česká pojišťovna (2.26 per cent). Korean Air explained its decision to exercise the option as part of its plan to reinforce its operations in Europe. Working together with the Czech partners in ČSA, the Korean carrier wished to make Vaclav Havel Airport in Prague its European hub. The participation of Travel Service in ČSA would provide Korean Air with connections to approximately 40 new destinations in Europe, to which its passengers would be able to fly after their transfer at Vaclav Havel Airport. As Travel Service would become a shareholder in ČSA, the Czech flag carrier would not lose the status of national carrier[2]. Soon afterwards, the Czech antitrust offices approved the transaction, followed by the European Commission. Therefore, the entire financial operation could be finalised in 2015.

This privatisation and the entrance of new partners was necessary to help ČSA survive. In 2013, the airline had made a loss of more than one billion Czech crowns (£33.8m) and had released around half of its total employees. Salaries of those who remained had been lowered by an average of 40 per cent. The airline had lost one-fifth of its passengers on scheduled flights, mainly due to its focus on Russia and other former Soviet destinations, which had been negatively affected by the Maidan Revolution in Ukraine in February 2014[3].

The restructuring of the carrier and privatisation did have a positive effect. In 2016, ČSA announced that it had returned to profit over the year 2015, recording an after-tax profit of CzK 241m (£8m). The carrier transported 2.26m passengers on scheduled flights and 2.7m passengers in total, including those on charter services. This was an increase of 13 per cent and 23.5 per cent respectively, compared with 2015.

In a move to obtain cash, ČSA sold its duty-free business. (Prague Airport)

ČSA obtained an Airbus A330 on lease from Korean Air. (Lukas Tochacek)

New Owners

Č SA attributed its turnaround to a positive operating profit in 2015 to the restructuring plan. This had included the reduction of the fleet, a headcount reduction, capacity cuts and load factor gains. Indeed, the load factor had improved from 67 per cent in 2014 to 72 per cent in 2015. Nevertheless, it remained below an industry average of about 80 per cent[1]. Notwithstanding these positive results, there was still a need for improvement.

First of all, after previous cuts, the route network had to be expanded again. Services to Helsinki were resumed in March 2016, followed by new or resumed routes to Birmingham, Kazan, Odessa, Ufa and Zagreb. In May, services to Pisa and Skopje were launched, with flights to Malta and Beirut following in June. In April 2016, ČSA announced it would be returning to the Arabian Peninsula after a break of several years, with the the intention of bringing Saudi visitors to the Czech spa resorts. At the beginning of July, the carrier started twice weekly flights to Riyadh, using an Airbus A319. At the same time, in agreement with Saudi Arabia, two ČSA Airbus A319s flew in Riyadh on behalf of Saudi Arabian Airlines. This way, the new summer schedule would include 47 destinations in 23 countries. Of course, the increased number of flights also required more aircaft for a six-month (summer) period. Therefore, ČSA rented Boeing 737-400 for Slovak carrier Go2Sky, while a fourth ATR 72-500 turboprop, leased for two years, would also enter the fleet[2].

Even taking this route expansion into account, ČSA's network remained predominantly European. Its only intercontinental route from Prague to Seoul ran in co-operation with a code-share partner and co-owner of the airline (Korean Air), whereas the routes to Abu Dhabi and the summer route to Riyadh were also operated with code-share partners. By country, ČSA's biggest market was Russia, which accounted for 20 per cent of its international seats on eight routes from the Czech Republic (from Prague to Moscow Sheremetyevo, St Petersburg, Rostov-on-Don, Yekaterinburg, Kazan, Samara and Ufa, plus from Karlovy Vary to Moscow Sheremetyevo). This was almost twice the 11 per cent accounted for by its second largest market, France, where it had only three routes (Prague to Paris CDG, Nice and Strasbourg). The third largest destination market was Italy; ČSA operated flights from Prague to Milan Malpensa, Rome Fiumicino, Bologna and Venice. ČSA now operated just three domestic routes, of which only one was situated in its own country. On the Prague–Ostrava route, ČSA was the only operator. In Slovakia, the airline operated a Bratislava–Košice flight and in Italy a Venice Marco Polo–Bologna route. These domestic routes in foreign countries were, however, part of multi-stage routes beginning and ending in Prague[3].

ČSA was the largest operator at Prague Airport, but its 18 per cent share of seats was very low compared with many other European flag carriers operating out of their main hubs. There were 12 low cost carriers (LCC) at Prague with a combined share of 31 per cent of the seats offered, including easyJet, Ryanair and Wizz Air. In addition, Travel Service was a significant operator at Prague. Although primarily a charter airline, it ranked third at the airport (after easyJet) by scheduled seats with an eight per cent share, and its scheduled services were flown under the SmartWings brand. ČSA had an extensive codeshare agreement with Travel Service, under which each partner carried the other's code on the majority of its routes from Prague[4]. Although the airline had continued its restructuring and expanded its network, it came as a surprise when ČSA announced, in 2016, that it had made a profit over the first half year for the first time in 12 years[5].

Besides expanding its route network, ČSA also changed its pricing policy in order to compete with the LCCs operating from Prague Airport. Starting with the summer season of 2016, ČSA came one step closer to low-cost carriers without actually becoming one, through offering low fares for passengers travelling with hand luggage only. Although these cheap tickets could not be cancelled, passengers could change the date of travel for a fee. For more expensive tickets, the limit for checked luggage was increased from 15kg (33lb) to 23kg (50lb). This offer applied to all destinations, with the exception of Seoul and Riyadh. ČSA hoped that these fares would give the company higher ranking on ticket search engines[6]. ČSA then went one step further some months later. Inflight meals were no longer included in the ticket price, but travellers who wanted a meal during the flight could buy one in advance. ČSA explained that it was no longer willing to include some muesli bars for a few crowns in the price of the ticket, but a good meal would be available for those who wanted to pay for it. This restructuring of ticket prices reduced costs to the customer by approximately 14 per cent compared with previous years, and the new tariff packages became more transparent to the passengers. Passengers preferring a comprehensive service would see comparable fares to a legacy carrier, whereas the budget-minded would see fares similar to low-cost operators. By the end of the year, ČSA could announce that it had carried 14 per cent more passengers than the previous year, albeit at a lower price. This growth was twice as fast as that at Prague Airport[7].

Saving an airline and leading it back to profitability cannot only be achieved by increasing income through increased ticket sales and expanding the network. Expenditure also has to be controlled. Therefore, ČSA sealed a deal, by which a large part of its future fleet would be leased rather than owned. Honouring the previous eight-year-old agreement with Airbus had proven untenable if ČSA's recovery was to be maintained. In 2008, prior to the financial and economic crash later that year, the airline had agreed to acquire seven Airbus A320 aircraft. Although the airline had returned to profitability by 2015, it could not afford to buy the new planes outright. The contract with Airbus was therefore revised; ČSA would buy a single aircraft of the latest A320neo version, while the remaining six aircraft of the original deal would be taken under an operational lease. This means the aircraft were basically rented by the airline without ownership, unlike financial leases where the assets are eventually transferred. The A320neos would replace ČSA's nine ageing and slightly smaller A319s. Both types are targeted at short- and medium-range routes. The new planes were to be delivered from 2019 onwards.

The airline's marketing strategy had evolved at the same time. The former concentration on mid-range connections with Russia and some of the states of the former Soviet Union had been reversed, with most new links focused on the Balkans or Western Europe[8].

Overall, 2017 was marked once again by good progress towards the revival of the airline. Transport indicators had improved. From the total of 2.9m passengers carried aboard its aircraft, 2.68m travelled on scheduled flights. The average load factor on scheduled flights had increased by almost six per cent to reach 81.1 per cent.

While ČSA itself had been restructured, Travel Service (shareholder in ČSA) also underwent major changes. On 18 September 2007, the Icelandair Group acquired a 50 per cent stake in the carrier and purchased further shares to bring its holding up to 80 per cent by April 2008. In December 2008, during the banking crisis experienced by Iceland, it reduced this holding to 66 per cent by selling shares to the other shareholders, including Unimex. By 2009, Icelandair's stake had been further diluted to 50 per cent through a new share issue, and the subsequent sale of a further portion to fellow owners brought this holding to 30 per cent. That 30 per cent stake was spun off into a new company that was later taken over by Icelandair's creditors, including the Chinese investment group CEFC China Energy, which obtained a 49.9 per cent stake in Travel Service[9].

In October 2017, Korean Air sold its 44 per cent stake in ČSA to Travel Service. Taking into account its previous investment in ČSA, Travel Service obtained a total of 78.7 per cent of the ČSA shares. If the Czech government decided to sell its own 20 per cent of the shares to Travel Service, this airline would secure a 97.7 per cent participation in ČSA[10]. A few weeks later, the Czech government did sell its shares to

Travel Service, pending regulators' approval. At that time, Travel Service was operating a fleet of more than 40 aircraft, including Airbus A320s, Boeing 737-700s, 737-800s, 737-900s and Cessna Citation business jets. As well as operating on Travel Service's charter flights, some of the aircraft were also used on regular scheduled flights under the Smartwings brand. For comparison, ČSA's fleet comprised 18 aircraft, including nine A319s, three ATR-42s and five ATR-72s, plus a single A330-300 on lease from Korean Air. Furthermore, the airline had seven A320neos on order that would replace some of the A319s once delivered[11]. Shortly after the takeover of ČSA shares, Travel Service announced it would transfer its branding from the airline to a holding company, and would move all of its operations under the Smartwings brand. The Smartwings livery would replace the Travel Service livery on its aircraft.

Travel Service Unimex became ČSA's largest shareholder. (Jozef Mols collection)

Travel Service Unimex became a holding company and its operations were carried out under the brand name 'Smartwings'. (Jozef Mols collection)

ČSA leased this Boeing 737 from Go2Sky. (SkyGTS Creative Commons Attribution-Share Alike 4.0 International, commons.wikimedia.org/w/index.php?title=File:OM-GTB_CSA.jpg&oldid=713750726)

Passengers who wanted a meal during the flight had to pay for the extra service. (Jozef Mols)

Chapter 14

COVID-19

Following the change of ownership in 2017, ČSA was pleased with the results over the first half of 2018. Passenger numbers increased by 22 per cent compared with the same period of the previous year. The airline could sign another interesting contract, in that Eurowings would rent up to five Airbus A319s from ČSA, for periods between 12 and 18 months. This low-cost subsidiary of Lufthansa would base the aircraft mainly in Stuttgart. As ČSA was planning to retire most of its older A319s anyway, this was a good way to move them on. Those Airbus 319s leaving the fleet would be replaced by Boeing 737-800s obtained from ČSA's owner Travel Service[1]. 2019 was also a good year for the Smartwings group, which as a whole had transported more than 9.6m passengers. ČSA had reported earnings before tax of CZK 79.2m (£2.7m).

Some more fleet changes were in the pipeline. ČSA's order of seven Airbus A320neos for 2021 delivery was changed in 2019 to four Airbus A220-300s and three long-haul A321XLR jets[2].

When the COVID-19 pandemic began, airlines around the world had to cancel flights and ground their aircraft. The same happened to ČSA. On 27 February 2020, its only long-haul aircraft, an Airbus A330 on lease from Korean Air and used on the code-share flight from Prague to Seoul in co-operation with that airline, had to be parked at Prague Airport. As the leasing contract for the aircraft would expire in October, it was very unlikely the A330 would still be used by ČSA after grounding[3, 4].

In May 2020, it was announced that ČSA would restart some of its operations after the lockdown was lifted. On 18 May, flights to Amsterdam, Frankfurt, Paris and Stockholm resumed. Six days later, operations to Kyiv, Odesa and Bucharest started up again. Passengers were required to wear face masks during the entire flight and a distance of 2m from person to person was advised. Furthermore, the cabin would be disinfected before and after each flight[5].

Naturally, the grounding of aircraft and cancellation of flights had a financial impact. As a result of the declaration of a state of emergency by the government of the Czech Republic and the introduction of extraordinary measures in connection with the spread of the virus, the Smartwings group had experienced a drop in flight performance of 95 per cent in the months of April to June 2020, and by more than 80 per cent in July and August. Therefore, Smartwings and ČSA filed a motion with the Municipal Court in Prague on 26 August to declare an extraordinary moratorium. The law, known as Lex Covid, was drawn up to mitigate the effects of the coronavirus epidemic and was cited in the airlines' request for a postponement of the maturity of their debts, while making it clear that they would not cease operations. All scheduled flights would be provided according to flight schedules, while other routes would return depending on the development of the epidemiological situation in individual countries and the status of their governments' accompanying travel restrictions. The moratorium would buy time for Smartwings and ČSA to ensure the financial stability of the company in co-operation with financing banks, aircraft lessors and other creditors[6].

Of course, ČSA and the Smartwings Group were not the only airlines to be hit by the pandemic. Around the world, hundreds of airlines faced financial problems. As a result, ČSA and Smartwings implemented a cost-saving programme and adopted every possible measure to mitigate the negative financial impact of the crisis, just like other airlines around the globe. However, while many foreign concerns had already benefited from the support of their national governments (for example, in the form of capital injection or provision of state-guaranteed loans), Smartwings and ČSA received no such aid until the COVID Plus programme, a package of support, was launched by the Export Guarantee and Insurance Corporation (EGAP) in the second half of July after notifying the European Commission[7]. In August, ČSA requested government financial support to cover 7,198 cancelled flights during the state of emergency in the period between 14 March and 24 May 2020 during which ČSA was forced to suspend its operation.

As a direct result of the pandemic, ČSA had suffered a loss of CZK1.57bn (£53m) and an unprecedented drop in the company's revenues to about 20 per cent of the previous year. Despite recommendations of the European Commission and the International Air Transport Association (IATA), ČSA did not receive any financial support from the government, unlike its competitors. Therefore, the airline was confronted with unequal and unfair competition[8]. As the Czech government did not assist its airline industry, ČSA and Smartwings had no other choice but to file for reorganisation according to the Insolvency Act. The application for reorganisation was filed due to the termination of the extraordinary moratorium and after exhausting all possible solutions to resolve the challenging financial situation caused by the global crisis. The aim was to save the company and to select the best possible solution for creditors. ČSA had already notified the Czech Labour Office that it intended to make mass layoffs[9], and of course, had to cancel the orders for seven next-generation narrow-body Airbus aircraft, including the A220 and A321XLR models. By the time this took place, the ČSA fleet was reduced to just eight aircraft, including a single A319, one A320, one Boeing 737-800 and five ATR-72-500s, which were grounded[10]. The Airbus aircraft were managed by lessor BBM, three of the ATRs were managed by ASL Aviation and the other two by Nordic Aviation Capital[11].

The reorganisation of the airline did see success. At a meeting, The carrier's creditors agreed to the reorganisation according to the plan proposed by Smartwings, under which ČSA would remain in business and gradually return to its pre-pandemic size. By that time, the court had recognised claims against ČSA in the amount of CZK821m (£27.6m). A new creditors' committee was also approved, including Česká spořitelna, UniCredit Bank, travel agency Fischer, leasing company Horizon Aviation, Flight Control, Czech Airlines Technics and, finally, Korean Air Lines. It also emerged from the meeting that the carrier had completely abandoned the possibility of state aid, though ČSA had negotiated with the Czech-Moravian Guarantee and Development Bank about possible compensation for the unused tickets and ČSA vouchers. According to a letter dated 4 June 2021, it was communicated by the Ministry of Industry and Trade that the concept of the bank guarantee or compensation of the state for unused flights would not be further developed[12].

Thanks to the entry of the newly founded company Prague City Air s.r.o, which is supported by Jiří Šimáně and Roman Vik, both shareholders of Smartwings, ČSA was saved. Prague City Air thus became a 70 per cent shareholder in ČSA, and Smartwings held the remaining 30 per cent. After the reorganisation, the shareholders could only come up with very cautious plans for the future. The company was planning to fly with only two leased A320s. If there was a buyer for the A319 aircraft, even for disassembly for spare parts, the company would sell it. Furthermore, the airline would only serve two destinations: Paris four times a week and Hurghada in Egypt three times a week[13]. In the future, it was planned that the airline would introduce four Airbus A220-300s into service.

In October 2022, the airline reconfirmed its intention to operate Airbus A220 equipment by 2024. In the meantime, the existing fleet of only two aircraft had been used extensively. Under ČSA route numbers, the A319 was used on flights to Paris, whereas for Smartwings, it operated flights to Malaga.

The A320 was used for a rotation to Hurghada for ČSA and to Antalya for Smartwings[14]. In June 2023, it was confirmed that ČSA would lease four A220-300s from Air Lease Corporation[15].

ČSA had survived the COVID pandemic and resumed operations, but in 2022 it suffered another major setback had to be countered in the form of the Russian invasion of Ukraine, which disrupted two of the strongest markets for Czech Airlines Cargo. In response to the conflict, activities were redirected to alternative markets. Since Czech Airlines Cargo was also the general sales and service agent for Delta International Airlines and Korean Airlines, it could establish robust feeder services for these carriers. Prague's strategic location at the heart of Europe, coupled with lower costs than its competitors, offered the company a compelling advantage[16].

For its winter 2023 schedule, ČSA announced two daily flights to Paris, two weekly flights to Madrid and two weekly flights to Yerevan, Armenia. Furthermore, passengers could reach more than 20 other destinations serviced by code-share partners.

It was clear from the beginning that the rescue operation for ČSA could only be a first step in a full-scale restructuring of the Czech aviation industry. In 2016, the Chinese state-owned company CITIC Group had acquired a 49.92 per cent stake in Smartwings, which owned 30 per cent of ČSA shares. The initial investor had been the CEFC Group, but its stake was taken over by CITIC after CEFC was declared bankrupt. Soon, however, the CITIC Group in turn wanted to sell its shares, but initial negotiations with Israir Airlines of Israel failed. On 20 February 2024, CITIC group finally sold its shares to Prague City Airport, which already held 70 per cent of ČSA shares. Prague City Airport had been founded by Smartwings Group owners Jiří Šimáně and Roman Vik. Once the deal was complete, Smartwings became a truly Czech-owned company. This would accelerate and facilitate further reorganisation.

In the summer of 2024, both Smartwings and ČSA announced that the ČSA brand would disappear that autumn. With the winter timetable, all ČSA and sister company Smartwings flights would be operated under the Smartwings code 'OS'. ČSA would thus no longer formally fly on its own account, but instead be considered as a wet lease provider for Smartwings. The abandonment of the 'OK' code therefore marked a symbolic step, signalling the end of ČSA's independent identity. Consolidating flights under a single code is intended to streamline operations and reduce costs, as well as helping to promote the Smartwings brand. The ČSA brand will not be written off completely, however. Two A320 aircraft will continue to fly in ČSA colours and will be joined later by four brand new A220-300 planes that should be delivered by the end of 2025. Even so, the two routes (Madrid and Paris), currently operated by ČSA, will be flown under the Smartwings 'OS' designation.

It is not yet clear what will be the consequences of these measures. Decisions such as these often lead to job losses. In any case, it is to be expected that ČSA will leave the SkyTeam Alliance, as it makes no sense to stay as a member. The airline will probably leave the alliance on the same day its loyalty programme ends. Since redeeming or using miles for tickets on other SkyTeam airlines will no longer be possible, Czech Airlines' membership in the alliance will become redundant.

There may be more changes in the pipeline. Rumours indicate that ČSA will become a holding company and a majority shareholder of Smartwings, but Czech-based Smartwings and its subsidiaries in Slovakia, Poland and Hungary would become the sole operating companies within the group. This would happen after a swap of shares, as the current owners of Smartwings and Prague City Airport might exchange their shares in their respective companies for shares in ČSA's holding. Ultimately, the ČSA brand would be preserved, not as an airline but rather as a financial institutional umbrella under which several carriers would operate. At the time of writing, this final decision has not yet been made.

A ČSA Airbus A319 logo jet. (Raymond Zammit)

This Airbus A320 received the special '100 years' livery. (ČSA Czech Airlines)

Accidents and Incidents

(Based upon information from the Accident Safety Network)

On 22 August 1930, Ford 5-AT-C Tri-Motor OK-FOR on a flight from Kbely Airport in Prague to Brno Turany Airport crashed in Jihlava. In poor visibility during a heavy thunderstorm, the aircraft made a sharp left turn to avoid a chimney, hit the ground and caught fire. Two crew members and 11 of the 12 passengers were killed.

On 13 August 1938, Savoia-Marchetti S.73 OK-BAG struck a wooded mountain near Oberkirch, Germany, on approach to Strasbourg, France. The aircraft was flying from Prague via Paris. All 17 passengers died; a stewardess survived the crash, but died a day later in hospital.

On 5 March 1946, Amiot AAC-1 (Junkers Ju 52/3m) OK-ZDN crashed near Prague while operating a flight from Paris with an intermediate stop at Strasbourg. The aircraft attempted to land twice at Prague Ruzyně Airport runway 22 and crashed on the third attempt; ten of the 15 crew and passengers died in the crash. The cause of the accident was an incorrect estimate of altitude by the pilot due to reduced visibility and insufficient equipment at the airport.

On 9 November 1946, Douglas C-47A OK-XDG force-landed near Dobrovíz after running out of fuel while in a holding pattern due to bad weather. All 18 on board survived, but the aircraft was written off.

On 24 December 1946, Douglas C-47A OK-WDD was written off following an emergency landing near Paris. All 15 people on board survived.

On 25 January 1947, Douglas C-47A OK-WDB was struck by a crashing Douglas Dakota while parked at Croydon Airport. There were no casualties, but the aircraft was written off.

On 13 February 1947, Douglas C-47A OK-XDU crashed shortly after take-off from Ruzyně Airport while on a ferry flight, killing all three on board. The aircraft had been acquired by ČSA from US military surplus; following delivery in Prague on 17 September 1946, it was overhauled and painted at Ruzyně Airport, after which it was to be flown to the Avia factory at Čakovice to install cabin upholstery and seats. Immediately after take-off of the ferry flight, however, the aircraft crashed. It appeared that the elevator control cables were reversed during overhaul.

On 6 April 1948, a Douglas DC-3 was hijacked to Neubiberg Air Base in Germany. The 17 passengers and three crew members wanted to leave communist Czechoslovakia.

On 21 December 1948, Douglas C-47A OK-WDN struck a hillside near Pylos, Greece, in bad weather, killing all 24 on board. It was flying from Prague to Lydda, Israel, with stops en route in Rome and Athens. The aircraft lost orientation due to cloudy weather and was circling Kalamata, where military operations were taking place at that time. There are conflicting reports about the circumstances of the accident; it has been suggested that the aircraft suffered a controlled flight into terrain due to poor weather. Other accounts say that when the pilot transmitted a flare, this was treated as a threat and the aeroplane was fired upon from the ground. A third account states that communist insurgents thought the aircraft was going to drop weapons, so they lit flares to signal a landing area for parachutes. The pilot thought the flares were outlining an emergency landing strip. As he descended, the aircraft impacted a hillside. In any case, all 24 people on board were killed.

On 27 February 1950, Douglas C-47A OK-WDY, operating a domestic scheduled service from Prague to Ostrava, struck Praděd Mountain. Six of the 25 people on board were killed.

On 24 March 1950, three Douglas DC-3s were simultaneously hijacked. The aircraft landed at the US Air Force base at Erding in West Germany. In all, 26 of the 85 passengers chose to stay in West Germany to escape communist rule in Czechoslovakia.

On 23 March 1952, a Douglas C-47 was hijacked by four people who demanded to be taken to Germany. The aircraft landed safely at Frankfurt with no casualties.

On 12 January 1954, Douglas C-47A OK-WDS struck a chimney and power lines and crashed near Prague after nearly failing to take-off. The aircraft was operated on a domestic scheduled passenger service from Prague to Ostrava. All 13 people on board were killed.

On 18 January 1956, Douglas C-47A OK-WDZ struck Mount Skapova after the aircraft was blown off course by strong winds. The aircraft was operating a domestic scheduled passenger flight from Bratislava to Košice. In total, 22 of the 26 occupants were killed.

On 24 November 1956, Ilyushin Il-12 OK-DBP crashed into a field near Eglisau, Switzerland, killing all 23 people on board. The flight was an international scheduled passenger flight from Zürich to Prague.

On 2 January 1961, Avia 14 OK-MCZ crashed on climb-out from Prague during a pilot-training flight, after failing to gain height on take-off. All ten people on board were killed.

On 28 March 1961, an Ilyushin Il-18V crashed in Gräfenberg, near Nuremberg, during a Prague–Zürich service due to structural failure, killing all ten people on board.

On 12 July 1961, Ilyushin Il-18V OK-PAF crashed near Casablanca-Anfa Airport, Morocco, due to possible crew error, killing all 72 people on board. The aircraft was performing an international scheduled passenger flight from Prague to Conakry in Guinea, with stops en route at Zürich, Rabat and Dakar. After leaving Switzerland, the crew contacted Rabat-Sale Tower and requested weather information for Morocco. Visibility was very low, so the flight advised it was heading for an alternate airport in Casablanca. Subsequently, the aircraft gave its position at five miles from Casablanca-Anfa Airport, requested permission to descend and asked for landing instructions. The crew was asked to call when on the downwind leg. Four minutes later, the flight was asked to call when on final approach and was told that it was number one for landing with a 4kt surface wind. The pilot replied that he would call when over the range station. The aircraft flew over the field and three minutes later, the pilot gave his altitude as 400m (1,300ft) and indicated a ceiling of 150m (500ft). The flight was advised that cloud was 7/8, ceiling 137–150m (450–500ft). Three minutes later, conditions were 7/8 at 100m (330ft). Subsequently, the crew asked permission to land at Casablanca Nouaceur Airport. Two minutes later, the tower asked the crew how much fuel was left. They replied they had enough for 90 minutes. While Anfa control was transmitting this request to the American authorities in Nouaceur, the aircraft crashed in line with runway 03, about 12.8km (eight miles) from its threshold. None of the assumptions of material failure, electrical failure, abrupt manoeuvre to avoid another aircraft or unfavourable weather conditions satisfied the investigating commission as being a definite cause of the accident. They assumed that, when the crew was warned about the deteriorating weather conditions at Anfa, they had decided to take advantage of the partial visibility of the ground between stratus clouds and had attempted a fast let-down in unfavourable conditions.

On 10 October 1962, Avia 14 OK-MCT crashed near Slavkov while on approach to Brno, killing 13 of 42 people on board. The plane was operating a domestic scheduled passenger service from Košice to Bratislava, Brno and Prague. Visibility at Brno was poor due to fog when the flight was cleared for an approach to runway 28. The aeroplane descended below minimum descent altitude because the pilot assumed he was closer to the airport. The plane impacted the side of Špidláky Hill.

On 16 March 1963, Tupolev Tu-124A OK-LDB caught fire and burned out while being refuelled at Santa Cruz Airport in India. There were no casualties, except for a flight attendant who was injured after jumping from the plane.

On 5 September 1967, Ilyushin Il-18D OK-WAI crashed on climb-out from Gander International Airport, Canada, while performing flight ČSA 523, linking Prague with Havana via Shannon and Gander. The flight took off from runway 14 to climb under an abnormally shallow angle. The highest altitude reached was 38m (125ft) at the end of the runway. It was a dark overcast night and the initial climb area, passing the runway end, was devoid of lights. The aeroplane then descended until it struck a wire of a mast before impacting the ground at a speed of 196 kt (363km/h). It continued until striking a railway embankment, 1,200m (4,000ft) past the end of the runway, and a post-impact fire broke out. No probable cause of the accident was determined. According to data available, the pilot-in-command's altimeter was subject to frictional errors, which might have resulted in slight delays in response and the pilot-in-command, and the co-pilot's gyro horizons were subject to pitch indication errors as a result of acceleration forces, which could have ranged from 1.5° to 4°. As a result, 37 of 69 people on board were killed.

On 11 October 1968, Avia 14-32A OK-MCJ crashed near Ptice shortly after take-off from Prague, killing 11 of 40 people on board. The aircraft was on a domestic scheduled passenger service from Prague to Košice.

On 1 June 1970, Tupolev Tu-104A OK-NDD crashed after two attempted approaches to Tripoli International Airport in Libya, killing all 13 on board. ČSA had introduced the scheduled service only a few weeks earlier, so the new crews had to familiarise themselves with the route and especially with the airports. Therefore, the composition of the crew was strengthened. There were three pilots in the cockpit (instructor, captain and co-pilot). The co-pilot was 'extra' in the cockpit and observed the flight from behind the pilot's seat. The instructor had landed at Tripoli only once before, but the other crew members had never been to this city.

On approach to Tripoli, the aircraft established contact with the tower and was cleared for a VOR approach to runway 18. However, the aircraft did not land. Instead, it made a fly-by, probably due to the high landing speed. Apparently, the crew had insufficient time to evaluate the development of the situation and at the same time control the plane so that it could land at the runway. The work was complicated not only by the lack of knowledge of the airport and the exact approach procedure, but also by the unfavourable weather conditions, with fog and ground clouds around the airport. So, after the fly-by, the Tupolev made a second landing attempt. The crew wanted to land on runway 01, but only runways 18 and 36 were operational, so the crew decided for a landing on runway 36. The tower responded: 'Understood, switching landing lights for runway 36, final approach to runway cleared'. They added that the safe height above obstacles for the runway was 143m (470ft). Then the plane made a low pass over the airport, turned in the opposite direction and entered the haze before the threshold of runway 36. The traffic controller at the tower was warned by an orange flash in the indicated direction, making it clear something had happened. The plane had crashed in the Fundok el-Sherif area, first touching down about 3.11m (5km) before the runway threshold. The undercarriage impacted first, then the wing, and over the next 400m (1,312ft), the aircraft gradually disintegrated. A fire then broke out in the wreckage of the hull, which definitively eliminated the chance of survival for any of the 13 passengers on board. Rescue units arrived at the scene of the crash almost an hour later.

The investigation showed that working with the Tu-104 was not an easy task. The planes lacked operational documentation, the location of devices and switches in individual planes differed from plane to plane and the devices worked with greater or lesser accuracies. Inspection of the accident site showed the plane broke apart on a relatively long strip, so it hit the terrain slowly, meaning the pilots had the plane under control until the last moment. After flying into the fog, they had lost their visual orientation and neglected the height. Examination of the bodies of the crew members showed traces of alcohol in the blood of the navigator, flight engineer and one flight attendant. It was not much, and probably did not affect their performance, but it said something about the airline's compliance with safety rules. Other problems were also discovered. Only the on-board mechanic had completed the mandatory pre-flight inspection at Prague Airport. The last time the navigator and flight engineer slept was about 18 hours before the accident, which could have had a negative impact on their attention spans. In the wreckage of the aircraft were found several-year-old, long-invalid air maps or flight documents for a navigation device that had not been in use for several months. The flight did not have a properly filled load sheet, a document that indicated the distribution and balance of the cargo in the plane. After the accident, however, it was found that the load and balance were correct[1].

On 18 August 1970, Tupolev Tu-104A OK-TEB landed wheels-up at Zürich Kloten Airport after the crew became preoccupied with cabin pressurisation problems. All 20 on board survived, but the aircraft was written off.

On 29 August 1973, Tupolev Tu-104A OK-MDE slid off the runway while landing at Nicosia Airport. All 70 on board survived, but the aircraft was written off. The probable cause was the failure of the pilot to stop the aircraft within the nominally adequate runway distance available and the subsequent entry of the aircraft into a right turn at high speed, as a result of which the aircraft was subjected to lateral centrifugal forces and skidded off the runway.

On 20 August 1975, Ilyushin Il-62 OK-DBF flew into the ground during a night-time approach to Damascus International Airport due to a misunderstanding between the pilots and the control tower that resulted in an incorrect altimeter setting. Only two of the 128 people on board survived. The aircraft was flying the Prague–Damascus–Baghdad–Tehran route. The atmosphere in the cockpit was not pleasant, as the pilots had personal problems and, according to some sources, were not on speaking terms. The co-pilot was not even supposed to be on the flight, but was called in at the last minute from standby to replace the original pilot, who did not show up for work. The autopsy of the captain of the doomed flight showed that he had been drinking alcohol prior to the disaster[2].

The flight proceeded completely normally. When the aircraft was three and a half hours in the air, it approached Baghdad and communication was established with the regional control centre, and then with the airport tower in Damascus. The crew received instructions for the descent and meteorological reports. It was a clear cloudless night. The co-pilot was flying the aircraft at that time; he confirmed the descent to flight level, reported a beacon flyover and initiated a right turn to approach the centreline of the runway. However, the crew did not announce the final phase of the approach when the plane descended directly to the runway. Five minutes after last contact with the control tower, witnesses reported a probable crash, some 16km (10 miles) northeast of Damascus Airport. As there were no roads leading to the crash site, the fire and emergency services did not arrive at the scene until 45 minutes after the accident was reported. The plane's black boxes were destroyed by the subsequent fire, but investigation of the wreck showed that the aircraft was equipped with several altimeters. The captain's altimeter was set to the correct pressure, and according to experts, was working correctly, but the captain was not flying the plane. The crucial instrument, the co-pilot's altimeter, was destroyed in the crash.

On 28 July 1976, Ilyushin Il-18V (OK-NAB), which was operating a scheduled domestic passenger flight from Prague to Bratislava, crashed in the Golden Sands (Zlaté Piesky) lake while attempting to land. Only three of the 76 people on board survived. The day before the accident, this aircraft had made a flight to Tripoli, Libya, with a defect noted on the left inner engine; oil had been leaking from the propeller speed reducer. During the night, the malfunction had been addressed and did not appear again. Just to be sure, ČSA sent one of the mechanics to Bratislava to check the engine again after landing[3].

The flight to Prague was routine, the problems only starting when the plane left the regional air traffic control and switched communication to the Bratislava centre. Thereafter, a chain of mistakes and misunderstandings led to the tragedy. The plane reported descending to flight level 90 (2,750m) but the controller ordered it to descend to flight level 80 (2,450m). No one noticed the misunderstanding. There was another problem; the aircraft was about 29km (18 miles) from the airport, but the dispatcher was mistaken and believed it to be 44km (27½ miles) away, which was why he didn't allow the plane to go down any further yet. The plane was thus 300m (984ft) higher than the dispatcher thought and 15km (9 miles) closer to the airport. It thus had to make a steeper descent too quickly, on a much shorter track. The crew tried to reduce speed by extending the landing gear and transitioning to a slight incline, thereby increasing the resistance of the aircrraft. Although the aircraft slowed, it gained altitude again. As a result, the Ilyushin descended at a speed of up to 22m/sec instead of the recommended 10m/sec.

At a distance of 2,700m (8,800ft) before the runway, the aircraft had a correct speed of 260km/h (140 knots); it was slightly off the runway, just above the glide slope, with landing gear extended and the flaps almost extended. To complete the approach, the crew had to increase engine power and increase the vertical rate of descent. Due to the stress the crew experienced during the wild approach, however, they did not react adequately to the situation, and instead of increasing power, the engine levers were moved to the ground idling position and the vertical speed did not change. The captain decided to abort the approach and repeat the circuit. The crew again increased power, but as a result of the previous reduction, engine no 3 automatically shut down. The engine stopped and the propeller blades automatically moved to the so-called flagging position. Subsequently, the mechanic made a fundamental mistake by pressing the wrong button, flagging engine no 4. As a result, the plane found itself without power on the right side and began to turn to the right in the direction of the Golden Sands lake. It narrowly missed the airport tower, but crashed into the lake, breaking up on impact with the water and quickly sinking. Only the tail part remained above water, in which four passengers were saved, but one of them died the day after.

On 2 January 1977, Tupolev Tu-134A OK-CFD collided on the runway at Prague Ruzyně Airport with a another ČSA aircraft, Ilyushin Il-18 OK-NAA, that was taking off. All 48 people on the Tu-134 survived but the aircraft was written off. In the Il-18, all six on board survived and the aircraft was damaged, although it was subsequently repaired and returned to service. Retired in 1981, it is now in a museum.

On 11 February 1977, Avia 14T OK-OCA struck trees and crashed near Bratislava Ivanka Airport due to crew error, killing four of five people on board. The probable cause of the accident was failure to follow the prescribed flight path and decision height in marginal weather.

On 11 October 1988, Tupolev-134A OK-AFB landed hard at Prague Ruzyně Airport. There were no casualties, but the aircraft was damaged. It was flown to Piešťany, where it subsequently served as a restaurant.

On 9 June 2012, ATR 42-500 OK-KFM was destroyed in a hangar explosion and fire at Ruzyně Airport. A second ATR-42, OK-JFK, was also damaged by the fire. Two ČSA Technics employees were working with an explosive liquid. The liquid was sucked into a heavy technics vehicle, which then blew up near the aircraft and caused the fire.

This Tupolev Tu-104 crashed near Tripoli on June 1970. (Alan Bushell)

Fleet Details

(Based upon information from ČSA, eng.wikipedia.org and planespotters.net)

Historical fleet

Aircraft type	Number used	Introduction to fleet	Removal from active fleet
Aero A.10	5	1923	1924
Aero A.14 Brandenburg	3	1923	1927
De Havilland DH.50	8	1925	1930
Ford Trimotor	1	1929	1930
Saro Cloud	1	1935	1938
Avia F-VIIb-3m	6	1936	1939
Savoia-Marchetti S.73	6	1937	1940
Junkers Ju 52	5	1946	1948
Junkers Ju 352	1	1946	1946
Douglas DC-3	7	1946	1956
Lisunov Li-2	8	1949	1957
Ilyushin Il 12	10	1949	1959
Avia Il-14	32	1957	1977
Tupolev Tu-104A	6	1957	1973
Let L-200 Morava	20	1958	1969
Ilyushin Il-18	18	1960	1990
Bristol Britannia	2	1962	1969
Tupolev Tu-124	3	1964	1972
Ilyushin Il-62	9	1969	1995
Ilyushin Il-62M	6	1969	1997
Tupolev Tu-134A	14	1971	1997
Yakovlev Yak-40	5	1974	1992
Let L-410 and L-410M Turbolet	12	1976	1981
Tupolev Tu-154M	7	1988	1999
Airbus A310-300	4	1991	2010
ATR 72-200	5	1992	2015

Aircraft type	Number used	Introduction to fleet	Removal from active fleet
Boeing 737-500	15	1992	2008
ATR-42-300	5	1994	2011
Boeing 737-400	15	1995	2016
ATR-42-400	2	1996	2005
ATR-42-500	6	2004	2018
Airbus A321-200	3	2005	2018
Airbus A319-100	8	2007	2022
Saab 340B	3	2008	2010
ATR 72-500	6	2012	2021
Airbus A330-300	1	2013	2020
Boeing 737-800	1	2018	2020

Current fleet

Aircraft type	Number	Delivery	Special stickers
Airbus A320-200	2	2020	*100 years* sticker

After receiving Il-12 and Il-14 aircraft, the Avia factory built the Avia 14 under licence. (Alan Bushell)

The Ilyushin Il-62 would remain the backbone of ČSA's long-haul fleet for a long time. (Alan Bushell)

The Tupolev Tu-134A was used on medium-haul routes. (Alan Bushell)

Yakovlev Yak-40. (Raymond Zammit)

The Tupolev Tu-154 was the last Soviet jet to enter the ČSA fleet. (Alan Bushell)

Notes and References

Chapter 1
1. 'Jan Kaspar', en.wikipedia.org
2. 'CFRNA', en.wikipedia.org
3. 'Julius Arigi', en.wikipedia.org

Chapter 2
1. 'Everything is OK', https://100.csa.cz/english/timeline/#/16763
2. 'Sandwiches or Broth?' https://100.csa.cz/english/timeline/#/16731
3. 'Welcome on board the Savoia Marchetti', https://100.csa.cz/english/timeline/#/16690
4. 'Beauty in the clouds', https://100.csa.cz/english/timeline/#/16667

Chapter 3
1. 'The Munich Agreement', en.wikipedia.org
2. ibid

Chapter 4
1. 'Hodek Hk-101', en.wikipedia.org
2. 'The Munich Agreement', en.wikipedia.org
3. ibid
4. 'Milestones in the history of U.S. Foreign Relations – The Yalta Conference 1945', United States of America Department of State, Office of the Historian

Chapter 5
1. 'ČSA as a state enterprise', https://100.csa.cz/english/timeline/#/16764
2. 'The 40s'; https://100.csa.cz/english/timeline/#16692

Chapter 6
1. Frommer, Fred, 'When Soviet-Led Forces Crushed the 1968 'Prague Spring,'' 14 March 2022, https://www.history.com/news/prague spring czechoslovakia soviet union
2. 'The 70s' https://100.csa.cz/english/timeline/#/16756

Chapter 7
1. 'The 70s,' https://100.csa.cz/english/timeline/#/16756
2. 'The 80s', https://100.csa.cz/english/timeline/#/16756

Chapter 8
1. 'The Velvet Revolution', en.wikipedia.org
2. 'Airbuses and Boeings', https://100.csa.cz/english/timeline/#/16675
3. ibid

4. ibid
5. 'The dissolution of Czechoslovakia', en.wikipedia.org
6. 'Slovak Airlines', en.wikipedia.org

Chapter 9

1. 'Air Ostrava', en.wikipedia.org
2. 'Silver Air', en.wikipedia.org

Chapter 10

1. 'Living with change', www.flightglobal.com, 1 January 2003
2. ibid
3. ibid
4. ibid
5. 'ČSA Czech Airlines joins Skyteam', www.avionews.it, 18 October 2000
6. 'ČSA management shake-up', www.businesstravelnewseurope.com, 19 April 2006

Chapter 11

1. 'A diamond in the emblem', https://100.csa.cz/english/timeline/#/16768
2. 'Smartwings', en.wikipedia.org
3. 'The 2007–2008 financial crisis', en.wikipedia.org
4. 'Annual analyses of the European air transport market, annual report 2008', European Commission, 5 May 2010
5. 'Development of ČSA's financial data from 2006 to the first half of 2011', *Official Journal of the European Union*, L92/16, 3 April 2013
6. 'ČSA Czech Airlines', en.wikipedia.org
7. Roberts, W, 'Aeroflot bids for ČSA', *Airfinance Journal*, 23 March 2009
8. 'ČSA Czech Airlines', en.wikipedia.org

Chapter 12

1. Cienski, Jan, 'ČSA gets Korean and Qatari suitors', www.ft.com, 5 December 2012
2. 'Korean Air bringing new key partner into ČSA Czech Airlines', centreforaviation.com/news, 5 December 2013
3. 'Travel Service becomes second biggest shareholder in Czech Airlines', english.radio.cz, 4 January 2015

Chapter 13

1. 'ČSA Czech Airlines: restructuring, partnerships and now growth for the SkyTeam's smallest airlines', centreforaviation.com, 2 November 2016
2. Sura, Jan, 'ČSA will start flying to Saudi Arabia, they will rent another plane', idnes.cz, 1 April 2016
3. 'ČSA Czech Airlines: restructuring, partnerships and now growth for the SkyTeam's smallest airlines', centreforaviation.com, 2 November 2016
4. ibid
5. Sura, Jan, 'Surprise: the nationalized ČSA is making money and getting more passengers', idnes.cz, 21 July 2016
6. Sura, Jan, 'ČSA will offer cheaper and more tickets without suitcases. They start flying to Iceland', idnes.cz, 29 November 2016

7. Sura, Jan, 'Head of ČSA: People have accepted paying for meals. We don't plan flights for a few hundred crowns', idnes.cz, 11 November 2016
8. Johnstone, Chris, 'Czech Airlines sets course to lease large part of future fleet', english.radio.cz, 30 March 2016
9. 'Smartwings', en.wikipedia.org
10. 'Korean Air steigt bei Czech Airlines aus', dpa-AFX., 6 October 2017
11. Nukina, Keishi, 'Travel Service to Acquire Korean Air's and Czech Government's Stakes in Czech Airlines', knaviation.net, 7 October 2017

Chapter 14

1. Eiselin, Stefan, 'ČSA tauscht Airbus A319 gegen Boeing 737 aus', aerotelegraph.com, 17 November 2018
2. Nowack, Timo, 'Czech Airlines geht mit A 321XLR auf die Langstrecke', aerotelegraph.com, 23 October 2019
3. Nowack, Timo, 'ČSA gibt einzigen Langstreckenflieger ab', aerotelegraph.com, 1 May 2020
4. Eiselin, Stefan, 'ČSA muss einzige Langstreckenverbindung stoppen', aerotelegraph.com, 4 March 2020
5. 'Czech Airlines to restart some flights after coronavirus grounding', arabnews.com, 9 May 2020
6. 'Smartwings and ČSA applied for a debt moratorium', zdopravy.cz, 26 August 2020
7. 'Smartwings and Czech Airlines are temporarily utilising the newly introduced extraordinary moratorium to alleviate the impact of the coronavirus pandemic and achieve a long-term sustainable financing solution', smartwings.com, 26 August 2020
8. 'Czech Airlines filed for reorganisation in the municipal court of Prague', aero-space.eu, 28 February 2021
9. Johnston, Raymond, 'Czech Airlines restructuring and laying off staff due to COVID crisis', expats.cz, 24 February 2021
10. Hardiman, Jake, 'Czech Airlines Airbus A321XLR & A220 orders cancelled', simpleflying.com, 6 August 2021
11. Cirium, 'Czech Airlines files for reorganisation', flightglobal.com, 26 February 2021
12. 'The state will not help ČSA. The creditors have approved their reorganization. Representatives of Korean Air also sat on the committee', zdopravy.cz, 9 June 2021
13. 'ČSA celebrated 99 years. When they exceed one hundred, they would also like to fly with Airbus A220-300s', airways.cz, 10 October 2022
14. Fabinger, Hakov, 'ČSA confirms intent to lease 4 Airbus A220s', simpleflying.com, 11 October 2022
15. Sipinski, Dominik, 'ČSA Czech Airlines to lease four A220-300s from ALC', ch-aviation.com, 8 June 2023
16. 'Czech Airlines Cargo: Evolving to meet expectations', aviation business news, 18 September 2023

Appendix 1

1. '1970: None of the pilots really knew the airport. The ČSA flight ended in disaster', Technet.cz, 10 June 2013
2. 'We've landed' he said and died. Only two survived the ČSA crash 36 years ago', Technet.cz, 19 August 2011
3. Series: the plane crashed into a swimming pool near Bratislava. It almost hit the control tower', Technet.cz, 28 July 2011

Other books you might like:

Historic Commercial
Aircraft, Vol. 7

Historic Commercial
Aircraft, Vol. 14

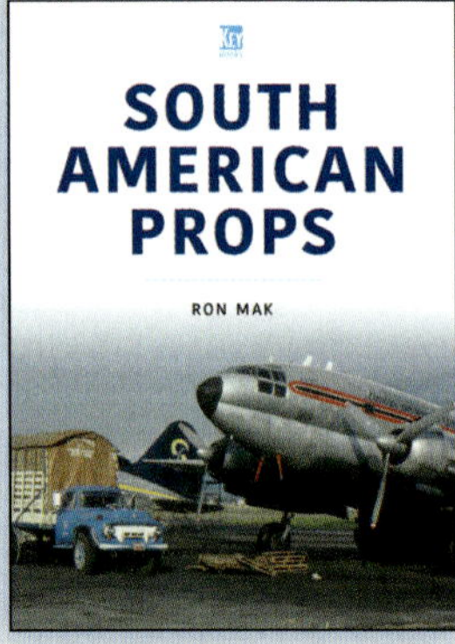

Historic Commercial
Aircraft, Vol. 15

Historic Commercial
Aircraft, Vol. 17

Historic Commercial
Aircraft, Vol. 18

Historic Commercial
Aircraft, Vol. 19

For our full range of titles please visit:
shop.keypublishing.com/books

VIP Book Club

Sign up today and receive
TWO FREE E-BOOKS

Be the first to find out about our forthcoming
book releases and receive exclusive offers.

Register now at **keypublishing.com/vip-book-club**

*Our VIP Book Club is a 100% spam-free zone, and we will never share your email with anyone else.
You can read our full privacy policy at: privacy.keypublishing.com*

Quirky

PETERBOROUGH

JUNE AND VERNON BULL

AMBERLEY

First published 2025

Amberley Publishing
The Hill, Stroud
Gloucestershire, GL5 4EP

www.amberley-books.com

British Library Cataloguing in Publication Data.
A catalogue record for this book is available from the British Library.

ISBN 978 1 3981 2349 6 (paperback)
ISBN 978 1 3981 2350 2 (ebook)

Typesetting by SJmagic DESIGN SERVICES, India.
Printed in Great Britain.

Appointed GPSR EU Representative:
Easy Access System Europe Oü, 16879218
Address: Mustamäe tee 50, 10621, Tallinn, Estonia
Contact Details: gpsr.requests@easproject.com, +358 40 500 3575